W0037916

# Restaurantes, rumba y más

# Restaurantes, rumba y más

## A Gringo's Guide to Latino Fort Worth

Peter A. Szok

TCU PRESS
Fort Worth, Texas

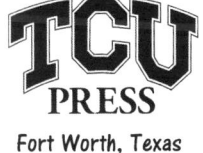

Copyright © 2014 Peter A. Szok

Library of Congress Cataloging-in-Publication
Data

Szok, Peter A., 1968-
 Restaurantes, rumba y más: A gringo's guide to
Latino Fort Worth / Peter A. Szok.
     pages cm
 ISBN 978-0-87565-598-7 (pbk. : alk. paper)
1.  Fort Worth (Tex.)--Guidebooks. 2.  Hispanic
Americans--Food--Texas--Fort Worth--Guide-
books. 3.  Hispanic Americans--Texas--Fort
Worth--Music--Guidebooks.  I. Title.
 F394.F7S96 2014
 305.868'07307645315--dc23

                                         2014011864

TCU Press
TCU Box 298300
Fort Worth, Texas 76129
817.257.7822
www.prs.tcu.edu
To order books: 800.826.8911

Design by Rebecca A. Allen

*For Busia and Dziadzia,*
*Agnes and Stephen Szok*

# Contents

# Acknowledgments

In writing this guide, I relied on the advice of several colleagues who work with me at Texas Christian University. Mark Villagran is a lifetime resident of Fort Worth and helped me to understand its older Latino elements such as boxing, lowriders, Tejano music, and Easter picnics. Flea markets and bargain hunting are two of Mark's passions, and his enthusiastic tales of weekend ventures set the agenda for my own wanderings. Felipe Barrios, who immigrated from Guanajuato in the 1980s, introduced me to such marvels as *sopa marinera*, shrimp cocktails, and *chamoyada* snow cones. Felipe is an aficionado of popular culture, and I benefited from his knowledge of Mexican film, festivals, music, and *jaripeo*. On one evening, early in my research, he gave me a magnificent tour of Plaza México, Fort Worth's center for Mexican rodeo. My Salvadoran friend José Henríquez (seen on page 3) acted as my guide to Latino nightlife. He pointed me in the direction of bars and discotheques and spent hours explaining trendy dress, drinks, norms, dances, and language. With his good humor and patience, José acted as my link to the bustle of younger generations. The staff of the TCU Press was equally helpful. I especially appreciate the assistance of Kathy Walton, Melinda Esco, and Rebecca Semik. Their efforts made this a better book. Finally, I would like to thank my wife whose many insights dot the text and who shares my enthusiasm for Fort Worth. On our first date, Cameron and I debated the merits of the city's Mexican restaurants. Presaging perhaps our imminent marriage, we immediately agreed that few things beat breakfast at Esperanza's.

*Above: South entrance to La Gran Plaza. Below: Aguas frescas at Esperanza's.*

# Fort Worth
## More than just "Cowboys and Culture"

"Cowboys and culture" is the slogan of the Fort Worth Visitor's Bureau, whose website touts the city's western history, its rodeo, its symphony, its honky-tonks, and Bass Hall, one of the leading opera houses of the Southwest. Of course, no one should forgo visiting such places as the Kimbell and the Modern Art Museums, with their impressive architecture and collections, their wonderful stores, cafes, and special exhibitions. It would be equally foolish to skip the Stockyards and a chance to witness the colorfully-patched longhorns as they lumber lazily down Exchange Avenue in the district's twice-daily cattle drive. The bulky beasts are a local icon and grace Fort Worth's flag and even its police cars. Nevertheless, the emphases on the frontier and on stunning galleries obscure other Cowtown realities, including a long-term immigrant presence and its equally significant legacies.

In *Stories from the Barrio*, Carlos Cuéllar delves into Fort Worth's Latino heritage, tracing it back to the early 1880s when a sprinkling of workers came from Mexico to take low-paying jobs in the recently opened rail yard. The Latino community

1

blossomed some thirty years later, after the start of the Mexican Revolution (1910-1920), which sent thousands of refugees across the border in search of peace and economic opportunities. Fort Worth's rail hub attracted transients, some of whom joined a plethora of Germans, Greeks, Poles, Italians, and Russians in the Northside's meatpacking industry. The Northside became the most important Latino barrio, while the Southside also drew in newcomers after its steel foundries opened in the early twentieth century. Today, over one-third of Fort Worth's population traces its ancestry to Latin America. Most Latinos are Mexican immigrants, or they are of Mexican descent. But there are also Salvadoran, Honduran, and Colombian minorities. Many families have resided here for generations, while others have arrived in recent years. The latter are the product of the social and economic turmoil afflicting Mexico and other parts of Latin America after the turn to free trade in the 1990s and the onset of deadly drug wars in the last decade. Violence and the North American Free Trade Agreement (NAFTA) have encouraged a new wave of immigration, dramatically transforming Fort Worth's population and putting into question its conventional identity.

If the Amon Carter and the National Cow-

*José Henríquez with his niece, Gabriela Cruz, at her quinceañera.*

girl Museums represent appealing aspects of the community, so too does the enormous **La Gran Plaza** mall (4200 South Freeway) with its *mercado* and thousands of weekend visitors who walk about its pleasant, park-like environs like people out for a Sunday stroll in Guadalajara. In the afternoon, mariachi bands enliven the environment with their instruments and heartfelt singing. And who could pass on La Gran Plaza's food court, which sells everything from Mexican *mariscos* to fruit salads, *elotes*, *mole*, *ceviche*, and *sincronizadas*, a quesadilla-like sandwich made of tortillas? **El Torito** serves Salvadoran *pupusas*, while the **Media Naranja** is one of the best places for *tortas* and *gorditas* in the city. What follows is a guide to these and similar enticements, intended to extend a gringo's vision beyond the cultural district's remarkable institutions, Sundance Square, and the famous Stockyards. I have grouped the venues into three categories: food, nightlife, and interesting places, and I have added a calendar with important events. Fort Worth is much more than "cowboys and culture," with a rich Latino heritage worthy of appreciation.

Above: East entrance to La Gran Plaza. Below left: Ballet Folklórico at Azteca de Fort Worth. Below right: La Glitter quinceañera store.

# Taquerías, restaurantes,
## and other dining options

**Pulído's** (2900 Pulido Street), **Mexican Inn Cafe** (2700 East Lancaster Avenue), and **The Original Mexican Eats Cafe** (4713 Camp Bowie Boulevard) are three of the city's oldest Latino restaurants and have long attracted the patronage of gringo customers. The Original opened in 1926 and became a favorite of Elliot Roosevelt, who lived in Benbrook in the 1930s and who introduced his father, FDR, to the business. Today a chalupa-enchilada-egg-taco amalgamation is named in honor of the president. **Joe T. Garcia's** (2201 North Commerce Street) is another longtime favorite, luring hundreds of patrons every weekend to its gardens and expansive buildings, which are modeled after a colonial hacienda. Joe T. Garcia's is a Fort Worth attraction, and while everyone deserves to sip a margarita next to the fountain on its lovely patio, this section proposes to expand horizons and to invite readers to establishments off the beaten gringo path. Among the suggestions are busy taco trucks, seafood diners, bakeries, and chicken joints as well as places for *menudo*, *barbacoa*, Mexican snow cones, sandwiches, gorditas, and *birria*. Wherever one goes, one can expect a good meal and perhaps a better understanding of Fort Worth.

*Pages 6-7: The enchanting patio at Joe T. Garcia's. Above: Homemade tortillas, a point of pride at Chalio's.*

*Fresh Tortillas and Goat Stew*
**Chalio Mexican Restaurant**
308 E. Seminary Dr.
Sun.-Thurs., 7 a.m.–10 p.m.; Fri.-Sat., 7 a.m.–2 p.m.
817-927-2400

2020 N. Main St.
Mon.-Thurs., 8 a.m.–8:30 p.m.; Fri.-Sat., 8 a.m.–
10 p.m.; Sun. 8 a.m.–9 p.m.
817-740-0465

Mexican chefs can be just as demanding about the taste of tortillas as the French are particular about the freshness of their bread and the Italians are scrupulous when selecting pasta. "The quality of the tortillas makes all the difference," insists Ricardo Luis, the owner of Chalio Mexican Restaurant with locations next to La Gran Plaza (4200 South Freeway) and on North Main, close to Marine Park. The California-based chain takes pride in its handmade corn tortillas, which are individually flattened and heated in an open kitchen so that clients can witness their fresh beginnings. Patrons pack Chalio's on Sunday mornings to select from an amazingly extensive menu, which leans more toward Mexico than toward Tex-Mex hybridity. Highlights include birria, a zesty goat stew which is dished up boneless or mixed with tendons and/or ribs. Another Chalio specialty is the *molcajete*, named after and served in the stone bowl traditionally used for grinding spices. The *Molcajete Azteca* combines grilled chicken, sausage, and beef with ranchero cheese, avocado, and a special chile sauce, while the *Molcajete Yucateco* adds a generous portion of shrimp. Both meals arrive blazingly hot, with the rumbling molcajetes continuing to smolder well after their appearance at the table. Chalio is one of the city's most Mexican restaurants and deserves the attention of more gringos who should also become familiar with **Birrería Jalisco** (3308 North Main Street), which is likewise known for its tortillas, excellent goat stew, and hospitality.

*La mangonada, one of the many delights at Chamoy . . . Puro Antojo.*

*Home of the Mexican Snow Cone*
**Chamoy . . . Puro Antojo**
707 W. Seminary Dr.
Daily 1 p.m.–10 p.m.

*Granadas, chirimoyas, aguacates,* and *zapotes* were a few of the amazing fruits devoured by Ilarione da Bergamo during a 1760s trip to Mexico. The Italian friar particularly enjoyed the prickly-pear cactus and gorged on its *tunas* until his urine turned red. Over the years, other travelers to Mexico have marveled and overindulged in the country's tropical produce, which is sliced and packed into plastic cups and sold on the streets like pretzels or hot dogs. Vendors add chile, salt, and lime juice to give the contents the spicy-sweet-sour quality so typical of Mexican desserts and candies. Mexicans eat massive quantities of fruit and blend it into *aguas frescas*, the non-carbonated drinks sold at restaurants. For an introduction to the aguas frescas and similar pleasures, check out Chamoy . . . Puro Antojo, a no-frills snack stand which opened in 2002 and which now has several kiosks around the city. Chamoy sells taquitos, churros, and elotes, and even a concoction called the Mexican Frito pie, but it is especially known for its fruit salads and *raspados* (snow cones), which are flavored with guava, melon, mango, and cucumber, among a dozen other options. The chamoyadas are the house specialty and fuse shaved ice, fruit, powered chile, and *chamoy* in an explosive combination. Chamoy is a zesty sauce akin to chutney. If you're on the Eastside, head to the exquisite **Frutería Cano** (1000 North Sylvania Avenue) which has a comparable menu.

*El Ancla (The Anchor) of NW 25th St.*
**Dos Molinas Mexican Restaurant**
404 NW 25th St.
Mon.-Wed., 7 a.m.–3 p.m.; Thurs.-Sat., 7 a.m.–9 p.m.;

Sun., 7 a.m.–3 p.m.
817-626-9394

If gringos are familiar with the businesses in the North Main and Hemphill areas, they are less acquainted with NW 25th Street and the Mexican eateries, *botánicas*, and ice cream shops that line this long and lively thoroughfare. The avenue is a Fort Worth treasure, yet it is strangely hidden from both tourists and locals. Anchoring the district, just blocks from the Stockyards, is the bustling Dos Molinas restaurant, which draws a loyal lunch and breakfast crowd and particularly hums on Saturdays and Sundays when extended families assemble around crowded tables. Dos Molinas is a Northside institution and tends to attract people from the surrounding neighborhood. The restaurant is the creation of Zack and Gloria Molina, who grew up in West Texas working the cotton fields, and who bring a sense of modesty to their cooking, which gravitates more toward Tex-Mex standards than toward traditional Mexican dishes. Some of the house favorites are *carne guisada*, daily menudo, mole, and barbacoa. Dos Molinas also serves pancakes and other American-style breakfasts. Customers praise the handmade flour tortillas. An internet reviewer advises, somewhat exaggeratedly, that if you're looking for a margarita, stick to Joe T. Garcia's, but if you "want a great meal, travel a quarter mile to a different world." On the Southside, **La Tortilandia** (1112 West Berry Street) and **Fiesta Mexican Restaurant** (3233 Hemphill Street) offer their clients equivalent food and surroundings.

*A taste of El Salvador*
**Fort Worth's Pupuserías**

Tex-Mex and Mexican are the prevalent orientations of most of Fort Worth's Latino restaurants; however, there are a sprinkling of other establish-

Pupusas *with* curtido *at the Torito.*

ments specializing in El Salvador's distinct cuisine. Fort Worth's modest Salvadoran population is a product of a bitter civil conflict that ravaged the Central American nation in the 1980s and sent thousands of refugees to the United States. While most landed in Los Angeles, Washington, DC, and New York, smaller numbers settled in Houston and Dallas-Fort Worth, bringing with them their beloved pupusas. The pupusas are fat corn tortillas, a legacy of El Salvador's indigenous population, which, like Native American groups throughout Mesoamerica, turned to maize as a basic source of nutrition. The thick dough patties are stuffed with pork, cheese, *loroco*, and refried beans. Loroco is an edible flower that tastes a bit like broccoli or asparagus and gives the pupusas an earthy flavor. Pupusas can be eaten plain or with *curtido*, a cabbage slaw with slices of carrots and onions. The Northside's **Market Latina** (233 NE 28th Street) is a popular spot for pupusas and other Salvadoran dishes. The restaurant also makes tamales, cassava, fried plantains, and soups typical of the Central American country. The **Torito Pupusería** (4200 South Freeway) in La Gran Plaza food court offers a very similar menu. **Doña Carmen Pupusería** is another option, with locations at 1712 North Sylvania Avenue and 1818 Hemphill Street.

*Joe T. Garcia's Worthy Companion*
**Esperanza's Mexican Bakery and Café**
2122 N. Main St.
Mon.-Sun., 6 a.m.–7 p.m.
817-626-5770
www.joets.com

With its high-ceilinged dining hall and worn tiles and chairs, Esperanza's tends to attract Northsiders whose families have been in Fort Worth for generations and who live in or who remain somehow connected to the neighborhood. On Sun-

*Breakfast at Esperanza's.*

days, the old timers drop in for a meal after mass
at All Saints Catholic Church. Esperanza's opened
in 1980 as an offshoot of the neighboring Joe T.
Garcia's. Its founder was Hope (Esperanza) Garcia
Lancarte, whose parents came from Michoacán in
the early twentieth century and opened a barbecue
for laborers in the meatpacking industry. Esperanza worked for years in her family's business and
helped to transform it from its humble beginnings
into one of the city's most iconic restaurants. She
envisioned Esperanza's as a more down-home eatery and initially prepared tacos, tortas, burritos, and
Mexican baked goods. The bakery and the unpretentious ambiance remain; however, Esperanza's
menu has expanded to integrate other things such

as mole, *chilaquiles*, *migas*, *flautas*, ceviche, sopa marinera, *milanesa*, and *caldos*. Specialties include *guisado*
in *chile verde*, *cabrito*, and green enchiladas. Esperanza's also has a wonderful patio, perfect for sipping a
fresh margarita. Esperanza's second location (1601
Park Place Avenue) is in the medical district, and
while it enjoys the same varied selections, it lacks
the old school charm of the North Main establishment.

*Barbacoa and Menudo*
**El Original Hernandez**
1617 NW 25th St.
Fri.-Sun., 9 a.m.-3 p.m.
817-626-8050

Barbacoa and menudo are longtime favorites
of many Fort Worth Latinos, who make these traditional foods at home and seek them out in local
restaurants, often on Saturday and Sunday mornings. Menudo is a spicy soup whose central ingredient is beef stomach, combined with hominy, oregano, and garlic, as well as chili, cilantro, and chopped
onions. Tortillas or *bolillo* bread accompany the
stew, along with a plate of lime or lemon wedges.
Menudo is thought to have curative qualities, including the ability to alleviate hangovers. Barbacoa
contrasts sharply with US barbecue and usually

involves the slow cooking of head meat, although almost any part of the cow can be used, with some preferring pork or lamb cuts. The beef is steamed or smoked until it is tender and is served on tortillas, in tortas, and in burritos. Most establishments sell these meals on weekends, given their clientele's insistence on freshness and the extensive time required for their preparation. Established in 1975, El Original Hernandez is thought to be one of the best places for menudo and barbacoa in the city. The restaurant focuses exclusively on these dishes and is only open on Friday, Saturday, and Sunday. Many people order takeout from El Original Hernandez, but others sit down and enjoy the chalet-like dining hall with its large windows looking out on NW 25th Street.

*Tex-Mex in an Enchanting Carport*
**Mi Cocinita**
3509 ½ Bryan Ave.
Wed.-Fri., 10:30 a.m.–2:30 p.m.
817-923-0033

The size and prominence of Fort Worth's leading Mexican restaurants obscure their modest and distant beginnings. In the 1930s, the Northside's Joe and Jessie Garcia began preparing lunches for hungry stockyard workers, creating the foundation for what later became the sprawling **Joe T. Garcia's** (2201 North Commerce Street). The Pulído family, whose franchises now stretch across North Texas, first made meals for railroad laborers in the hardscrabble *El TP* barrio. Similarly, Southside housewife Betty Mendez opened her kitchen under her carport in 1967. Betty specialized in burritos and enchiladas and churned out tamales for the holiday season. Fortunately, less has changed at Betty's than at **Pulído's** (2900 Pulido Street) or at Joe T. Garcia's. Virgie Martinez, Betty's daughter, took over in 1987. The carport was enclosed, and a small courtyard added, but Mi Cocinita (My Little Kitchen) remained faithful to Betty's vision, providing Tex-Mex favorites in a cozy environment. Patrons walk down a flower-lined driveway

*The walkway (driveway) to Mi Cocinita.*

to reach the charming dining area decorated with ceramics and dangling chile lights. Outside, a pecan tree shades the patio, affording guests with another pleasant seating area. Today Betty's grandchildren and their spouses manage Mi Cocinita, carefully preserving Fort Worth's most singular eatery. For those who take delight in its intimate atmosphere, **Amy's Restaurant** (1537 North Main Street) provides another snug setting for Mexican food and hospitality.

*A passion for freshness*
**Paco & John Mexican Diner**
1116 8th Ave.
Mon.-Fri., 7:00 a.m.–2:00 p.m.; Tues.-Fri., 5:30 p.m.–
9 p.m.; Sat., 9 a.m.–2 p.m., 5:30 p.m.–9 p.m.
817-810-0032
www.pacoandjohn.net

In his discussion of recipes and identity, historian Jeffrey Pilcher notes that in the mid-twentieth century, many Mexicans were reluctant to give up their daily jaunts to the market in favor of refrigerating their perishables. They understood, as their predecessors had before them, that freshness was a central characteristic of good cooking. This ethos is readily apparent at the Paco & John Mexican Diner, a whistle-clean establishment in the medical district and a favorite hangout for doctors and nurses and for the hipster denizens of the nearby Fairmount neighborhood. Paco & John is located in an overhauled gas station, and with its retro signage and drink coolers, it evokes a vaguely Austin-ish ambience. No alcohol is available, but you can BYOB and even sit on an enclosed patio. Seating inside is also available, but you need to arrive early, especially at lunchtime. The diner is the vision of Francisco Islas and Bernard Tronche. Tronche is

*Francisco Islas, your gracious host at Paco & John.*

the longtime owner of **Saint-Emilion** (3617 West 7th Street), a prominent French restaurant where Islas was employed for many years. Tronche and Islas named their eatery in honor of their eldest children and committed themselves to delicious and affordable cuisine. Most breakfast and lunches are under seven bucks, while dinners generally range from nine to fifteen dollars. The French and Mexican cooperation generates what a reviewer depicts as delightful additions to familiar dishes. Slices of roasted peppers grace shrimp quesadillas. The "street tacos" can be ordered with succulent red snapper, and among the various breakfast options is an unexpected salmon burrito. Weekly specials are particularly creative and have included such things as duck enchiladas, trout *a la veracruzana*, and pork *huaraches*. Whatever you request, you can be assured of superior quality, as freshness is Paco & John's signature ingredient.

Paleta *carts await their cargos outside La Flor de Michoacán.*

## Paleteros, Popsicles, and La Flor de Michoacán
North, Central, and South Fort Worth

Travelers in Latin America of different periods have frequently underlined the importance of street vendors, whose shouts or *pregones* draw the public's attention and who have been portrayed in movies, music, and literature. "El Manisero" is a famous Cuban song that replicates the pronouncements of a Havana peanut seller. Fort Worth residents are never subjected to the elongated trumpeting of "*maní*," but they do hear the soft jingles of the city's ice cream peddlers. Dozens of *paleteros* cruise the north and south sides mounted on bicycle carts and ringing small bells. Not surprisingly, they tend to congregate near playgrounds. The paleteros sell Jolly Ranchers, Sour Wowers, and comparable products, but also delicious, locally-made popsicles. The *paletas* are cream or water-based and are typically mixed with seasonal fruits such as strawberry, mango, guava, cantaloupe, and tamarind. Freshness is essential to a good paleta. **La Flor de Michoacán** is the city's main competitor, but other producers participate in the trade. If you find yourself outside their principal routes, go to the **Clinton Place Nevería** (2423 Clinton Avenue), which has a wonderful selection of homemade paletas. Further west, **Realeza Michoacana** (1600 NW 25th Street) offers an equal variety of choices. Most ice cream shops take their name from Michoacán, as Tocumbo, a small town in the western Mexican state, is widely credited for developing the popsicle.

*Mexican baked goods and more*
**Panadería La Fe**
4210 Hemphill St.
Mon.-Sat., 6 a.m—10 p.m.
817-924-1153

If corn was indigenous to pre-Hispanic Mexico, wheat arrived with the Spanish Conquest and for years remained associated with Europe, wealth, power, and social privilege. Historian Jeffrey Pilcher notes how colonial bakeries relied heavily on forced labor, while their products were largely rejected by native people and consumed by Europeans and their descendants. Pilcher even observes that young dandies sometimes advertised their status by sprinkling crumbs on their collars. If wheat's elitist associations remain evident in the rolls at expensive Mexican restaurants, it is also clear that bread has become a staple for a much wider range of sectors. This expansion is apparent in the neatly arranged display cases at the Panadería La Fe, one

*Drive-through window at Panadería La Fe.*

of Fort Worth's most beloved Mexican bakeries. The enterprise produces over two dozen baked goods, including *yoyos, conchas, novias, moños, bolillos,* croissants, *campechanas, troncos, tornillos, orejas, cemitas, polvorones,* and *roles de canela.* Regulars rave about La Fe's empanadas, which are generously stuffed with pumpkin, yams, and pineapple. La Fe (The Faith), which has served the Southside for over two decades, also cooks tortas and burritos for lunch. Stop by before the Day of the Dead to pick up the popular *pan de muerto* (bread of the dead), a sweet roll shaped in a cross and bones. For Epiphany, La Fe makes *rosca de reyes,* a round fruit cake with a tiny doll, representing Jesus, buried inside it. Fort Worth has other impressive panaderías, including the Orduno family's **Anakaren Bakery** with locations at 4242 McCart Avenue, 8751 Camp Bowie West Boulevard, and 1308 North Sylvania Avenue.

*Roasted chicken tempts the senses at La Gran Plaza's south entrance.*

*Marinated, grilled chicken*
**El Pollo Regio**
4200 S. Freeway
Sun.-Thurs., 9:30 a.m.-10 p.m.; Fri.-Sat., 9:30 a.m.-11 p.m.

817-923-4595
www.elpolloregio.net

715 N. Riverside Dr.
Sun.-Thurs., 9 a.m.-10 p.m.; Fri.-Sat., 9 a.m.-11 p.m.
817-831-2366

If NAFTA and neoliberalism propelled Mac-Donald's and Burger King to open franchises across Latin America, they also encouraged Mexican fast-food chains to establish themselves in the United States. One example is the marinated, grilled chicken business pioneered by El Pollo Loco in the 1970s. El Pollo Loco began as a traditional food stand in the Sinaloan town of Guasave. Its owner Juan Francisco Ochoa recognized Mexicans' passion for open-air barbecues and developed a model for serving flame-roasted chickens in more formal but economical restaurants. By the early 1980s, El Pollo Loco was penetrating California, following the path of Mexican immigrants who appreciated the food's familiarity and freshness. El Pollo Regio is a spinoff of this earlier success. Founded in 2002 by Juan Jorge Bazaldua, it began without fanfare in a trailer in Austin. Currently the franchise has locations across the Metroplex, Oklahoma, and other parts of Texas. Like its competitors, El Pollo Regio strives to maintain the spirit of the roadside kitchens. A juicy *pollo entero* (whole chicken) goes for just $12.98 and comes with tortillas, beans, rice, and a grilled onion. Generous two-piece and half-chicken dinners are also available, along with soups, burritos, and tacos. The term *regio* is derived from *regiomontano* and refers to Bazaldua's native city of Monterrey. On the Northside, **El Pollo Cachuchón** (1101 NW 28th Street) features a similar menu. In Scenic Bluff, **Super Pollo** (805 North Sylvania Avenue) is another excellent choice.

*The spacious Nuevo Leon restaurant.*

*The Tastes of Villaldama in Fort Worth*
**Restaurant Nuevo Leon**
1544 Ellis Ave.
Tues.-Sat., 10 a.m.-10 p.m.; Sun., 9:00 a.m.-9:00 p.m.
817-625-0757

The González family opened the Nuevo Leon in 2006 in a small storefront facing Marine Park. Today the restaurant accommodates its guests in a spacious and pleasant environment, reminiscent of the eateries off Mexican plazas. The tiled dining area features colorful paintings and seating with ample room between tables, along with several flat-screen televisions innocuously broadcasting Cowboy games, the Mavericks, or other sporting events. The Nuevo Leon has a well-stocked bar and is a terrific place to sip a *michelada* while watching broadcasts of Mexican league soccer. The michelada is a Bloody Mary-like concoction, mixing *cerveza* (beer), lime juice, and dashes of soy with Tabasco and Worcestershire sauces. The drink goes down like a spicy punch. The locale also boasts delicious ceviche, shrimp platters, fish, and other seafood dishes. Customers praise the sopa marinera, the tilapia fillets, and catfish dinners. Before immigrating from neighboring Nuevo León, the Gonzálezes operated a *cabrito* (kid goat grill) in their hometown of Villaldama. In Fort Worth, they employ this experience to prepare savory steaks, fajitas, and other broiled meats. Roasted kid goat and *machitos* (goat innards) are prepared regiomontano style. Plan to go on Sunday mornings, when the Nuevo Leon sells Mexican breakfasts and mariachi groups arrive to perform for tips. The musicians are often high school students and play with enthusiasm and remarkable talent.

*Pre-Hispanic Legacies and Roasted Corn*
**Ricos Nachos y Elotes 'El Toro'**
In front of Fiesta Mart, 2700 8th Ave.
2 p.m.-9 p.m. daily, except Wed.

A Náhautl song to the goddess of nourishment presents her revealingly as an assemblage of maize. "Oh Seven Cobs of Corn," sings the hymn to Chicomecoatl, ". . . arise now, awaken . . . You are Our Mother." Corn was the most important staple of pre-Hispanic Mesoamerica and was a part of daily sustenance, religious life, and festivals. It would survive the Spanish Conquest and an invasion of pigs, cattle, horses, and wheat-eating Europeans to remain a central aspect of the Mexican diet. Not surprisingly, corn is a familiar snack in Fort Worth's Latino neighborhoods. The

*Preparing* elote *at El Toro.*

word "elote" is derived from *elotl* (a Náhuatl term) and translates as corn on the cob. The elotes are boiled or grilled in their husks and splattered with a swirling array of condiments. Toppings include mayonnaise, butter, Parmesan cheese, sour cream, lime juice, and chile powder. One of the best spots to eat elote is outside the 8th Avenue Fiesta Mart, at the tiny *'El Toro'* stand. There the corn kernels are cut from their cobs and served in convenient Styrofoam bowls. The adventurous should grab an *elote con todo* (with everything) and take a stroll about Fiesta Mart, an interesting store where loud recordings entertain shoppers with a jumble of *rancheras*, *norteñas*, country, and rock hits. Elote vendors are found in other parts of the city. La Gran Plaza **Fiesta Mart** (421 West Bolt Street) has a kiosk, as does **El Río Grande Supermarket** (3037 South Freeway), on Saturdays and Sundays.

## A Few of Fort Worth's Taco Heavens
## Taquerías

The appropriately named **Arco de Noé** (Noah's Ark) sells a startling variety of food items in its humble and tiny confines at the corner of Primrose and North Sylvania Avenues. Burritos, tortas, tacos, and quesadillas are the standard fare at taquerías, which also provide an array of meat choices, such as *asada* (grilled steak), *carnitas* (shredded beef or pork), fajitas, *lengua* (beef tongue), *chicharrón* (pork rinds), pollo (chicken), barbacoa (steamed beef), and chorizo (sausage). *Tripas* (intestines), *guisado* (stew), *buche* (pork stomach), and *cabeza* (beef head) are a few more of the options. **El Mil Tacos** (3910 Hemphill Street), **Ernesto's** (4050 Hemphill Street), and **Juanito's Taquería** (4150 Hemphill Street) are three of the best places to indulge in these delicacies, especially after a

*Menu board at Melis Taquería.*

CARNITAS
BARBACOA
LENGUA
BISTECK
CHICHARRO
FAJITA CHI
TACOS AL
SABADO y D

second shift or a late night on the town. Located within blocks of one another, the restaurants remain open until the early morning hours and produce Mexican-style eggs for the breakfast crowd. On the Northside, **Eva's Taquería** (3401 North Main Street) cooks up many of the same selections in a bare-bones, mid-twentieth century diner. Further south is the cheerfully lit **Taquería Acapulco** (1515 North Main Street), an open-air stand with covered picnic tables and a view of the surrounding neighborhood. Close by is the legendary **Granny's Tacos** (703 East Long Avenue), serving giant homemade tortillas stuffed with pork, beans, potatoes, cheese, and salsa. Granny's creations really are more burritos than tacos. On the Westside, **Melis Taquería** (4304 West Vickery Boulevard) has its enthusiastic supporters and is especially worth visiting for its avocado sandwich. **Guajardo's** (1703 NW 28th Street, #B) and **Taquería San Luis** (1901 8th Avenue) specialize in *tacos al pastor*, a legacy of Middle Eastern immigration to Mexico, featuring marinated pork grilled on a vertical spit. Also keep an eye out for Fort Worth's ubiquitous taco trucks. **Salsa Limón** (2916 West Berry Street) is a TCU favorite with its "mothership" located at La Gran Plaza (4200 South Freeway).

*Tortas and gorditas*
**El Metate**
1705 NE 28th St.
Mon.-Tue., 6 a.m.-3 p.m.; Wed.-Fri., 6 a.m.-5 p.m.;
Sat., 8 a.m.-5 p.m.; Sun., 8 a.m.-2 p.m.
817-624-0900

On most afternoons, the parking lot outside El
Metate (the grinding stone) hums with the com-
ings and goings of customers whose hustle con-
firms the locale's widespread reputation as one of

Gordita de barbacoa *at El Metate.*

the best spots for tortas in Fort Worth. The torta is a bursting Mexican sandwich which comes in a crusty, oval-shaped baguette and is packed with chicken, steak, sausage, and other meats. Probably the most distinctive aspect of the torta are its sundry and tasty garnishes which give it a juicy, almost burrito-like quality. Mayonnaise, onions, avocado, and tomato are some of the most typical toppings, along with refried beans, lettuce, and jalapeños. El Metate prepares several dozen versions of the savory tortas. The gordita or "little fatty" seems like the torta's distant cousin, smaller and less flamboyant but delivering the same punch. The thick corn cake is cooked on a griddle and is crammed with an assortment of meats and vegetables. Beef and chicken stews, marinated pork, and diced nopales are some of the common fillings, as are eggs, potatoes, and sausage. **El Metate** is a great choice for gorditas and tortas and provides its clients with an exceptional view of downtown. **La Media Naranja** (4200 South Freeway) is another option, with wonderful fruit salads, yogurts, juices, and *sincronizadas* in its impressively extensive menu. The sincronizada is a tortilla sandwich comparable to the quesadilla.

*Freshly made tortillas at La Nueva de Zacatecas.*

*Recreating home, one tortilla at a time*
## Tortillerías

Collaborating with indigenous informants and artists, the sixteenth-century friar Bernardino de Sahagún (1499 –1590) produced the *Florentine Codex*, a massive investigation of pre-Hispanic Mexico, its religion, government, and social and economic structures. A revealing passage from the text relates the story of a female slave who had been captured in battle and forced from her community. Interestingly, she takes refuge in her cooking, in kneading maize dough and grilling tortillas. Historian Camilla Townsend notes how the "hearth and the *metate* (mealing stone)" helped to shape this woman's identity and how they would "comfort her anywhere and everywhere" she went. This same logic seems apparent in Fort Worth, where immigrants have opened multiple tortillerías and through them have forged a similar feeling of belonging. **Tortillería La Nueva de Zacatecas** (4241 McCart Avenue) cranks out fresh tortillas every morning and welcomes its customers with a sense of familiarity. La Nueva has several other locations around the city (1513 NW 25th Street, 831 North Sylvania Avenue, 3700 Decatur Avenue) and serves economical breakfasts and lunch plates. Its North Sylvania store is especially inviting, with a simple yet pleasant area for dining. **Ibarra's Tortillería** (1109 NW 25th Street) operates on a similar model, selling fresh corn and flour tortillas as well as tacos, tamales, flautas, and other light fare. **La Superior Tortillas y Más** best illustrates this capacity to recreate home in a new context. La Superior is located at 923 East Seminary and operates out of what was once a Sonic drive-in. If you're on the Westside, go to **Tortillería La Original de Zacatecas** (7931 Camp Bowie West Boulevard), a lively little spot, especially on Sundays.

*The Glory of Mexican Seafood*

**Vallarta's**
1108 W. Seminary Dr.
Mon.-Thurs., 11 a.m.-9 p.m.; Fri., 11 a.m.-10 p.m.;
Sat.-Sun., 10 a.m.-10 p.m.
817-923-9444

The Aztecs' island capital arose in the middle of Lake Texcoco, which once covered much of the Valley of Mexico and where the metropolis of Mexico City lies today. The lake, which was drained during the Spanish period, afforded resources to the Aztecs, who also established far-reaching trade networks that connected the city to the Gulf Coast and supplied them with octopi, snails, clams, and lobster. Upon arriving in 1519, Cortés marveled at the "great quantities of fish—fresh, salt, cooked and uncooked," available in the Aztec markets. Ceviche, scallops, crabs, and oysters are a few of the delicacies at Vallarta's and a reminder of this important influence on Mexican cooking. Vallarta's is famous for its sopa marinera, which combines a lavish mix of seafood items with vegetables in a spicy broth. Vallarta's Mexican seafood cocktails are also excellent, with extravagant servings of shrimp or octopus swimming in a tangy tomato sauce, along with cilantro, avocado, and onions. The cocktails come in tall chilled glasses with saltine crackers for scooping out their contents.

*Above: Sea-themed murals at the Acapulco Restaurant. Next page: Waiting for the bull at Plaza México.*

While Vallarta's draws throngs on a daily basis, there are other options for Mexican seafood, many of which are enchantingly decorated with paintings of mermaids, dolphins, whales, and other creatures. The **Acapulco** (1320 NW 25th Street) and the **Mariscos Restaurant** (1401 NW 25th Street) sit just a block from one another and vie for clients with their eye-catching murals. Both have impressively extensive menus, with things as varied as red snapper and frogs' legs. The Acapulco bustles on weekends with the aid of a playful pianist. The nearby **Acapulco Beach** (2612 Ephriham Avenue) offers much of the same cuisine, with a second location at 3112 North Main Street. **La Playita** (3025 Cleburne Road) competes with Vallarta's in south Fort Worth and hosts late-night transvestite shows on Saturday evenings. East of I-35, visit **El Puerto de Acapulco** (1025 East Seminary Drive), which has a well-deserved reputation for excellent fish dinners.

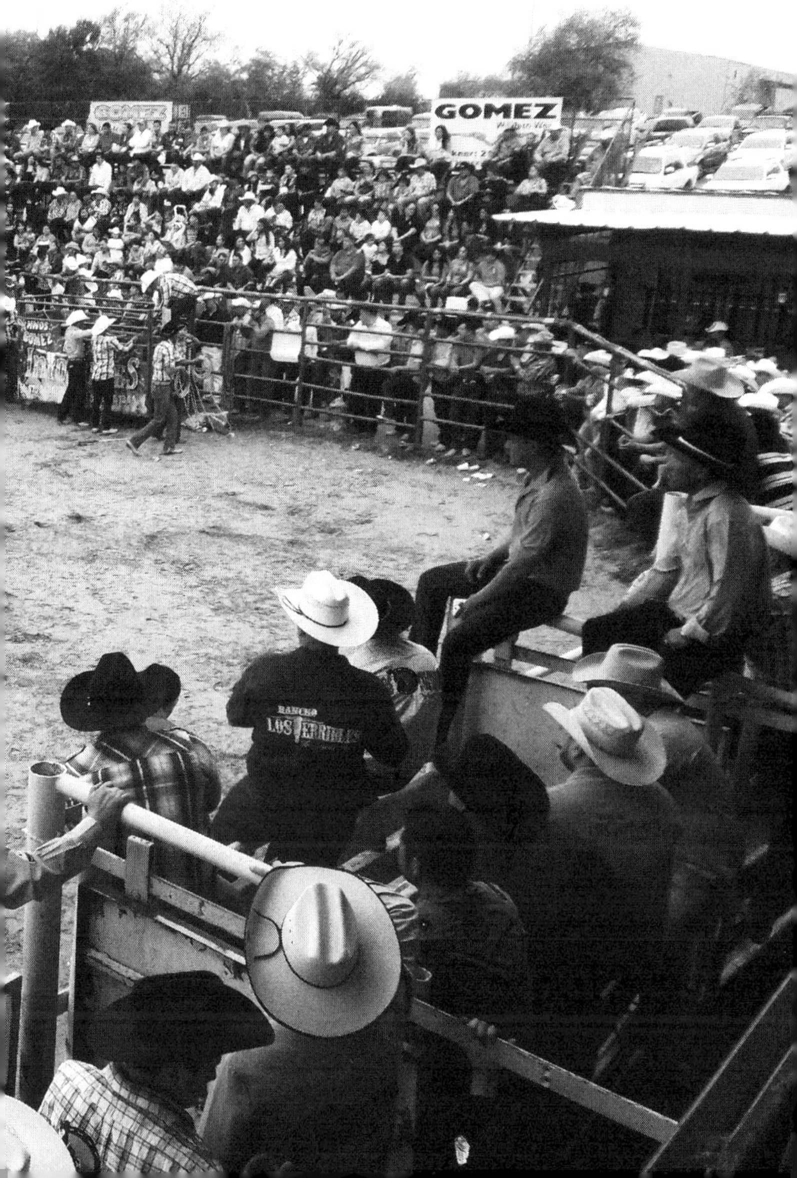
GOMEZ

# Lugares interesantes
## Interesting Places

With the support of the Fort Worth art commission, sculptors David Newton and Tomás Bustos recently erected a bronze Mexican cowboy at the corner of North Main Street and Central Avenue. The vaquero sits proudly on his powerful mount, dressed in a charro outfit, honoring Mexican contributions to the cattle industry. The Northside statue, which stands at the entrance to this Mexican American neighborhood, is one of the few formal

recognitions of Fort Worth's Latino population. Unfortunately, Latinos remain largely absent from the city's monuments and official identity; nevertheless, they increasingly dominate its everyday life, its amusements, cuisine, and popular culture. Below is a list of interesting places that reflect this ongoing and historic presence. Barbershops, botánicas, rodeo grounds, and markets probably do more than concrete and metal markers to illustrate the Latino presence in Fort Worth.

*Misa en español*
## All Saints Catholic Church
214 NW 20th St.
Mass Schedule: Sat.: 7 p.m. (English), Sun.: 7 a.m. (English), 9 a.m. (English), 10:30 a.m. (Spanish), 12 p.m. (English), 2 p.m. (Spanish), 6 p.m. (Spanish)
817-626-3055

Located in the heart of the Northside neighborhood, All Saints has long stood as an important institution of the Fort Worth Latino community. The parish was founded in 1902 and initially catered to the European immigrants who came to work in the meat-packing industry. After World War II and white suburbanization, All Saints took on its Latino character and ultimately came under the direc-

*Father Stephen Jasso of All Saints Catholic Church.*

tion of the Franciscans and Father Stephen Jasso. Jasso, who arrived in the mid-1990s after extended service in Peru and Mexico, is a steadfast defender of Latino rights and an articulate critic of the current anti-immigrant climate. He has worked hard to expand All Saints' social and educational mission while depending heavily on *jamaicas* (fundraisers) to meet the church's budgetary needs. Major events include the annual *Cinco de Mayo* carnival and the September commemorations of Mexican independence. In December, All Saints hosts a Christmas *posada* celebrating Joseph and Mary's trip to Bethlehem. Consider attending the Sunday, 6 p.m. mass when the chapel brims with the communal spirit, typical of Latin American Catholicism. Father Ángel Infante, who directs this service, inspires with his eloquence and calls for forgiveness. Other Catholic parishes catering to the Latino community include: the **San Mateo Mission** (3316 Lovell Avenue), **Immaculate Heart of Mary** (201 Thornhill Drive), **Holy Name of Jesus** (2635 Burchill Road), **St. George** (3500 Maurice Avenue), and **Our Lady of Guadalupe** (4100 Blue Mound Drive). The diocesan web site (www.fwdioc.org) lists the churches and mass times.

*Artesanías*
**Amigo's Pots & Crafts**
1117 N. Main St.
Mon.-Fri., 9:30 a.m.-6 p.m.; Sat., 9:30 a.m.-5 p.m.
817-624-2007

With roots in the colonial and the pre-Hispanic periods, Mexico's craft industry bloomed in the mid-twentieth century after intellectuals, inspired by the country's revolution, rejected an agenda of Europeanization and embraced the vernacular as national culture. *Artesanías*, or handicrafts, now became conspicuous in Mexican paintings, movies, and literature, and they emerged as a part of an increasingly important tourist sector. Today, Mexico

*Earthenware frogs at Amigos Pots & Crafts.*

City's massive Mercado de la Ciudadela welcomes thousands of foreign travelers who purchase textiles, baskets, and comparable objects as mementos of their stay in the capital. Many of these items are also available in the United States, as free trade has provided new markets for artisans and for those who attempt to replicate their works in less traditional, more industrial settings. Amigo's Pots & Crafts in Fort Worth offers an excellent selection of handmade goods, including clay planters, *jarrones*, and garden statuary; *talavera* platters, cups, plates, and vases; rustic chairs, tables, mirrors, and other furniture; folk paintings; tiles; and religious items. Dozens of *chimeneas* line the outdoor patio, along with whimsical earthenware frogs, rabbits, pigs, and other animals. Amigo's opened in the early 1990s and initially operated out of a battered bus. Today, the enterprise retains an air of humility, with workers greeting customers with unusual hospitality. For a similar introduction to artesanías, visit Fairmount's **Old Home Supply House** (1801 College Avenue). For rustic furniture, try the **San Carlos Imports** website (www.sancarlosimports. com). San Carlos is based in Fort Worth and offers a great variety of products.

*Haircuts and histories of the Northside*
**Ayala's Barber Shop**
1537 N. Main St., #B
Mon.-Sat., 8 a.m. - 5 p.m.
817-626-1672

With their local ties, camaraderie, and friendly discussions, barbershops convey a sense of community, less perceptible in other parts of the city. For a better grasp of the Northside, stop by Ayala's, which opened its doors in 1954 and which charges just $9 for a haircut accompanied by a pleasant introduction to the neighborhood. Louis Ayala is a longtime Fort Worth resident whose parents immigrated from Guanajuato in the early twentieth century and settled in Texas after a brief stay in Indiana. Ayala began trimming hair at age fourteen, in a barbershop where he had worked as a shoeshine boy. His boss Jack Mead paid for his training, and in honor of this generosity, photos of Mead and his wife are displayed on the walls. Close by hangs a portrait of Paulie Ayala, who in 1999 won a world boxing title and whose feat was celebrated with a raucous parade passing in front of his uncle's store. Ayala takes pride in his nephew's accomplishments, in his community, and in his profession. Clients over the years have included the rich and famous, including actors Brian Dennehy and Jason Robards, who sought out Ayala's services while working in the Metroplex. On most days, however, more humble customers sit in the benches at Ayala's, waiting

*Carmen Uribe, longtime barber at Ayala's.*

patiently for their haircuts and filling the room with their warmth and banter. For a similar experience, venture to **Boyo's Barber Shop** (1423 NW 25th Street)—or head to **The Barber** (1264 West Magnolia Avenue) for a more youthful environment with a jukebox and a well-worn pool table.

*Bajito y Suavecito*
**Lowriders and Fort Worth's Cruising Scene**
Weekends on Hemphill & N. Main Streets

"Low and slow" is the slogan of the drivers who cruise about town in their eye-catching vehicles with whitewall tires and elaborate rims, polished chrome bumpers, and showy paint jobs. Many of the automobiles also possess hydraulic systems that allow them to "dip" or "hop" in extravagant fashion. As their name suggests, lowriders travel unusually close to the ground due to alterations in their suspensions. Like the zoot suit phenomenon, the lowrider craze blossomed in the mid-twentieth century, as a means for working-class men of Mexican descent to dispute their marginalization and call attention to themselves. Although lowriders remain a distinctly masculine diversion, they now attract people of varied ethnic backgrounds. The vehicles circulate on North Main on Friday

*Bel Air lowrider on the Northside.*

and Saturday evenings and are displayed on the Southside at the **Hemphill Street Carwash** (3636 Hemphill Street). Parks are another point of congregation, especially **Echo Lake** (900 Echo Lake Drive), east of I-35, where dozens of lowriders periodically gather on weekends and occasionally duel one another in rowdy hop competitions. Holidays are the time to see the vehicles, as the Majestics, the Carnales, and other auto clubs organize special exhibits for the public. Diamond Hill natives Jason and Robert Little cater to the lowrider enthusiasts at their immaculate body shop, **The Station** (2000 North Main Street), which is decorated with Texaco signs and other memorabilia.

*Botánicas*

**Marisol's Mystic Shop**

2833 Hemphill St.

Mon.-Fri., 11 a.m.-7 p.m.; Sat., 11 a.m.-4 p.m.

817-921-9571

The botánicas manifest a range of influences, reflective of Latin Americans' approach to the spiritual. Much like the Day of the Dead celebrations, the *botánica* is a product of cultural syncretism and mixes orthodox Christian perspectives with indigenous and African religious and cura-

*Pope Francis among the pantheon of botánica candle saints.*

tive practices. These establishments normally sell Catholic statuary, rosary beads, candles, medallions, and amulets, along with a variety of herbal treatments, ointments, perfumes, baths, teas, and other folk cures for maladies ranging from diabetes to stomach pain, arthritis, menstrual discomfort, and asthma. Other products are available for less physical ailments such as unemployment, financial troubles, depression, and heartache. Many botánicas employ *curanderos/as* who give advice on natural remedies and who sometimes perform palm and card readings or who conduct special healing rituals. Marisol's Mystic Shop opened in 1980 and is one of the city's most complete botánicas. If you find yourself intrigued by alternative treatments, also consider consulting one of the city's *sobadores*. Sobadores practice a form of massage therapy and address things such as backaches, sciatica, sprains, tension, and migraines.

*Post-NAFTA cowboys and the bota picuda*
**Gomez Western Wear**
2765 Ellis Ave.
Mon.-Sun., 9 a.m.-8 p.m.
817-740-7999

Skinny jeans, rhinestone belts, cowboy hats and shirts are a few of the accoutrements of the pierced and tattooed youths who crowd into Latino dance halls on weekends and who follow the example of their *pachuco* predecessors, using flamboyance to dispute their marginalization. If the zoot suit defined the pachuco look, the *botas picudas* are the most iconic marker for this new wave of immigrant hipsters. The pointy boots are a transnational creation. They are a post-NAFTA adaptation of rural footwear, forged on both sides of the US-Mexican border, and worn for dancing to *tribal* (trē-bal), a hybrid genre which fuses European techno music with *cumbia* and other traditional rhythms. To wear the botas is to embrace the ambivalence that characterizes globalization and the

*A relatively modest bota picuda.*

immigrant experience. The outrageous boots are works of art, adorned with eye-catching patterns and decorations. Many even sport electric lights that glow in the darkness of the *discoteca*. Their most distinguishing characteristic, however, is their extreme length, with the narrow toes extending, in some cases, to the shoulders. The best place to see the botas picudas is on the dance floor at **Escapade 2001** (2401 South Campus Court) or the **OK Corral** (4200 South Freeway). If you can't escape on a Saturday evening, visit one of the city's Mexican cowboy shops. **Gomez Western Wear** (2765 Ellis Avenue) has a large selection of belts, hats, buckles, shirts, and boots, including the extravagant botas picudas.

*Traditions of Elegance*
**The Master Tailor**
3020 Stanley Ave.
Mon.-Fri., 9 a.m.-5:30 p.m.; Sat., 9 a.m. -1 p.m.
817-926-4221

In a society characterized by ethnic and social breaches, clothing in Latin America helps to indicate one's position, marking important economic and cultural divisions and allowing a temporary way to traverse these boundaries through refined

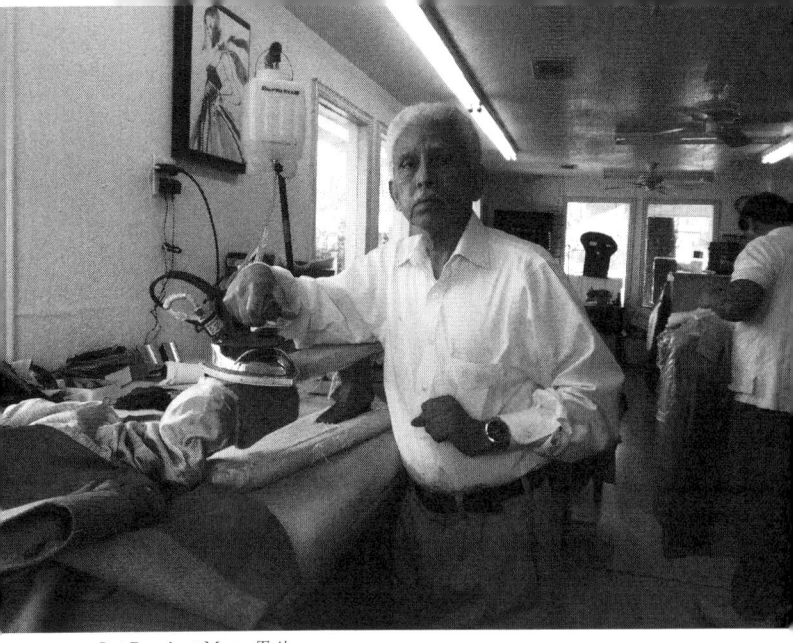

*José Parada at Master Tailor.*

taste and a fashionable outfit. In the Spanish colony, clothing's function as a status symbol encouraged the development of tailors and seamstresses whose talents were especially cherished by elites who craved the fashions of their European counterparts. Historian Marie Francois notes how in the mid-nineteenth century, even as manufactured clothing was becoming common, Mexico City professionals sought out tailors whose services they considered a mark of distinction. In Fort Worth, this appreciation for fine attire is readily evident at Master Tailor, a Latino-owned establishment and one of the few locales still capable of making handmade apparel. Master Tailor furnishes its clients with affordable alterations, the kind of adjustments done by area dry cleaners, but it also boasts two expert craftsmen who produce custom bridal gowns, suits, and blouses. José Parada opened Master Tailor in 1987 after years of work at Jack Howard Men's Wear, which catered to Fort Worth's wealthiest families. Parada had emigrated from El Salvador, where he had taken up the trade when he was just twelve. In the United States, he introduced his sons to the profession, and they now labor proudly alongside their father.

*Colonial Mexico in a Suburban Mall*
**La Gran Plaza**
4200 S. Freeway
Mon.-Sat., 9 a.m.-9 p.m.; Sun. 10 a.m.-8 p.m.
817-922-8888
www.lagranplazamall.com

La Gran Plaza opened in 2004 and quickly became a social center for the area's Latino population. Its designers at the California-based Legaspi Company refurbished the faded Town Center Mall and converted it into an imitation Mexican city, complete with towers, kiosks, and wrought-iron

benches, and a series of courtyards for live entertainment. *Paleteros,* or popsicle vendors, sometimes
circulate about the building, adding to its remarkable ambiance. La Gran Plaza has its own mariachi
academy, and guest artists, a house *trío,* and *ranchera*
groups stage performances on Saturdays and Sundays. Programming is also provided on holidays
such as Mexican Independence Day and Cinco de
Mayo. The businesses at La Gran Plaza range from
Burlington Coat Factory to a bingo hall, a cinema,
and medical and dental clinics. There are *quinceañera*
and Mexican western-wear shops, photo stores, ice
cream parlors, and even an airbrush art studio. Vis-

*Monster jungle gym in La Gran Plaza food court.*

itors are encouraged to enter the multistory *Mercado* where dozens of merchants sell their products inside tiny vending stalls. The Mercado houses tailors, hair stylists, and spiritualists, a travel agency, and a minuscule internet cafe. The Mercado is also an ideal place to buy candy; indeed, several stands are packed with Mexican sweets. The lower level opens to a large food court with a massive jungle gym and an abundance of dining options. La Gran Plaza is at its best on the weekends, when hundreds of families crowd into the building and recreate the feel of old Mexico.

## Jaripeo (Bull Riding)
### Plaza México

*Opening ceremonies at Plaza México.*

1000 Oak Grove Rd.
Weekend afternoons from spring through fall

Most Fort Worthians have gone to the city's famous Stock Show, which runs from mid-January to early February, or they have attended the weekly and more modest rodeo held at the quaint Cowtown Coliseum. Far fewer have been to Plaza México, the ramshackle complex located in south Fort Worth, where from early spring into the fall, Mexican horsemen put on exhilarating exhibitions of a dangerous sport known as *jaripeo*. Jaripeo is a form of bull riding that evolved in the colonial period following the Spanish introduction of cattle. Today, jaripeo is enthusiastically practiced across Mexico and in parts of the United States. Contestants mount bulls and charge out of familiar bucking chutes; however, the cowboys often do not use their hands but brace themselves only with their legs. They attempt to stay on for as long as they can, preferably until the animal tires and several rope handlers secure it with lassos. Jaripeo is a boisterous affair and takes on the air of a rural festival with food vendors, dancing, and musical performances. Brass bands play continually during the action and stir the bulls and crowd with their trumpets, crashing cymbals, tubas, trombones, and

drums. Plaza México hosts jaripeo on the weekends, with announcements airing on radio stations such as **La Raza** (93.7 FM) and **La Bonita** (106.7 FM). Brightly printed handbills are another form of advertisement. Look for them in Mexican stores and restaurants.

*Baseball on the Northside*
**La Liga del Norte**
Rockwood Park
748 Rock Crest Dr.
Weekends, March through October

Like soccer, boxing, and thoroughbred racing, baseball came to Latin America in the late nineteenth century as part of its growing ties to the international economy. US sailors, engineers, railroad workers, and businessmen introduced the game after traveling to the region to attend to burgeoning foreign investments in mining, transportation, commerce, and export agriculture. Meanwhile, wealthy Latin Americans ventured northward, studying in US schools and universities and often becoming enthusiastic fans of *béisbol*. Latin American baseball began as an elite activity; however, it quickly spread to other sectors and became deeply integrated into local culture. Today it is the national pastime of Puerto Rico, Panama, Venezuela, Cuba, and Nicaragua and is immensely popular in parts of Mexico. This legacy is apparent in Rockwood Park where *peloteros* gather from March to November to compete in Fort Worth's Liga del Norte, one of several adult baseball associations in the area. Founded some twenty-five years ago, La Liga

*Team Granjenal takes the field at Rockwood Park.*

claims among its alumni Yovani Gallardo, the star of the Milwaukee Brewers, who occasionally stops by after finishing the Major League season. Take in a game in October when hundreds of fans attend the playoffs and create a rowdy, festive environment. La Liga members are a welcoming bunch. Don't be surprised if someone hands you a beer, a coke, or even a plate of food. Game times are announced on the league's Facebook page.

## Fort Worth Muralismo
## Manuel Pulído

Mexican *muralismo* dates back to the pre-Hispanic period, when artists decorated temples and aristocratic residences with religious and historical imagery. If the tradition declined during the colonial era, it was reborn in the 1920s, when as part of a broad cultural reevaluation associated with the Mexican Revolution, Secretary of Public Education José Vasconcelos commissioned David Alfaro Siqueiros, Diego Rivera, and José Clemente Orozco to adorn the walls of government buildings with indigenous and nationalist themes. Muralismo soon spread into the United States, inspiring Depression-era artists to undertake similar projects commissioned by the Works Progress Administra-

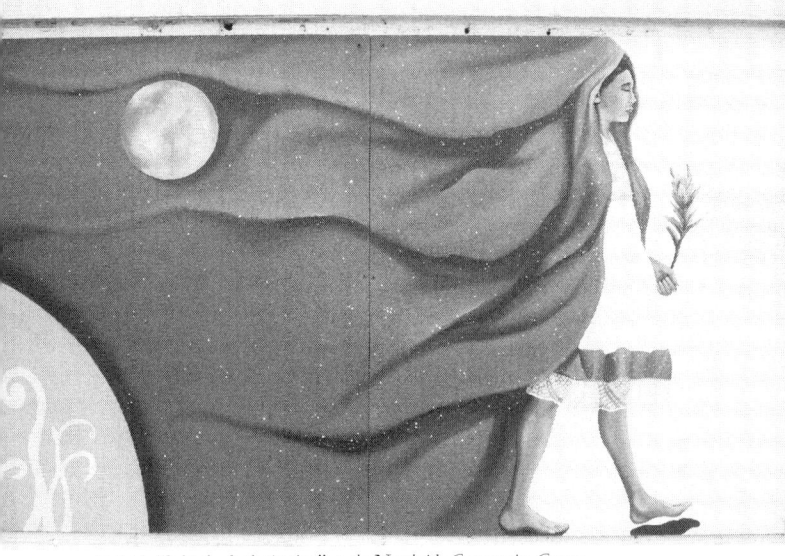

*Pulído's "Rebirth of Aspiration" at the Northside Community Center.*

tion (WPA). In the 1970s, the Mexican American community embraced muralismo as part of the Chicano movement. Fort Worth naturally did not escape these influences and developed its own tradition of mural painting. Today its main exponent is Manuel Pulído, a member of the well-known restaurant family who studied art at the University of North Texas and whose commissions have taken him across the country. Locally, Pulído's murals appear in the **Northside Community Center** (1100 NW 18th Street) and in the **César Chávez** (3700 Deen Road), **J. P. Elder** (709 NW 21st Street), and **M. G. Ellis Schools** (214 NE 14th Street). He recently restored Anthony Domínguez's paintings at the **Northside Branch Library** (601 Park Street). Pulído is a proud son of Fort Worth whose creations often reflect local themes.

## The Mexican *Tianguis* (Market) in Fort Worth

In a 1520 letter to Charles V, the Spanish conqueror Hernán Cortés glowingly described the market of the Aztec capital, marveling at its size, its order, and its products. The Spaniard recorded merchandise as diverse as jewelry, snails, eagles, pigeons, vegetables, timber, eggs, fish, dogs, and bedding. Barbers and restaurateurs intermingled among the traders, and there was a section specifically for herbs and medicinal products. The *tianguis*,

Levanta pompis *(butt-boosting) jeans at a Fort Worth tianguis.*

or bazaar, survived the conquest and flourished during the colonial and national periods as a place where plebian women contested the frequently exaggerated conventions of Latin American patriarchy. Today women still dominate these public spaces. In the final decades of the twentieth century, the traditional markets grew in importance as Mexico implemented neoliberal economic policies and its citizens struggled amidst massive unemployment. The tianguis is a kind of Mexican Big Lots, as becomes apparent strolling about Fort Worth's **Pequeño México** (950 North University) or the **Henderson Street Bazaar** (1000 North Henderson Street). Both venues feature dozens of vendors hawking everything from toothpaste to dining room tables. The North Henderson location is especially impressive, with a plethora of mechanics and others providing services. Indeed if you're looking for someone to tint your car windows, the Henderson Street Bazaar might have a few options. Thousands of shoppers arrive on the weekends and create a festive atmosphere. Pequeño México even has a rustic cantina with *norteño* bands playing amid the smell of roasting chicken. If you find yourself charmed by the aromas and bustle, plan to go to La Gran Plaza's **Mercado** (4200 South Freeway), with its dozens of indoor peddlers and a gigantic dining area. **Treasure Island Trade Days** (6250 Old

Hemphill Road) also has a distinctive tianguis feel and occasionally hosts Mexican musical groups. On the Northside, head to the **Long Bazaar** (318 East Long Avenue) for bargains and an engaging experience on Saturdays and Sundays.

## Moorish Traces and the Urban Hacienda

Moorish forces occupied the Iberian Peninsula from 711 to 1492, leaving behind an enormous cultural heritage, some of which made its way to America. Among the Arab-Berber legacies to arrive with the Spanish conquest of Mexico was the architectural importance of the patio. On the frontier, the enclosed courtyard afforded protection and fulfilled a need for separation in a society preoccupied with female honor and purity. In describing his psychological formation, the Mexican poet Octavio Paz recalled how he grew up behind "adobe walls," while beyond lay a "valley, a mountain . . . the neighbors' patio." The same impulse to ground oneself in encircled space is evident in Fort Worth's Latino communities, as TCU professor Bonnie Frederick has noted in a recent study. Newcomers to the city's older, central neighborhoods often build brick walls around their houses or surround them with fancy wrought-iron fences, many of them crafted by **Ibarra Welding** (3723

*La Playa Maya Restaurant (3200 Hemphill St.) features the urban hacienda look.*

Hemphill Street). The buildings themselves can take on a hacienda-like appearance with showy inlays, arches, and other additions. Even where no actual barriers appear, the front lawn might exude an oasis-like quality with dense trees, shrubbery, lawn ornaments, and potted plants. Probably the best spot to see these creative structures is between 8th Avenue and Hemphill Street, from West Berry to West Seminary. If you find yourself fascinated by the metalwork, take a look at **Efrain Gutierrez**'s website (www.efrainironart.com). Gutierrez is a local welder who makes whimsical iron sculptures.

*The King of Supermercados*
**El Río Grande**
3037 S. Freeway
Mon.-Sun., 7 a.m.-10 p.m.
817-769-7000
www.elriogrande.net

El Mariachi, the Monterrey, Fiesta, and El Rancho are a few of the grocery stores that have established themselves in Fort Worth in response to the growing immigrant presence. Among the most appealing of these enterprises is the Río Grande Latin

*Produce section at El Río Grande supermarket.*

American Market, a Dallas-based chain with seven locations in the Metroplex and with a large and devoted customer base. On weekends, the Río Grande takes on a fair-like ambiance with face painters and clowns providing amusement for children and loud *banda* music blasting over the sound system. Like its competitors, the Río Grande targets patrons who are familiar with the amenities of traditional markets and who especially appreciate its piles of fresh produce, colorfully arranged below dangling piñatas. Workers churn out tortillas in the morning, along with bolillos, empanadas, and other baked goods. The establishment receives high marks for its sweet breads and its enormous flan and *tres leches* cakes. A taquería and grill prepare terrific lunches and slow-cooked barbacoa on the weekends. The Oasis Juice Bar is a wonder unto itself with delicious fruit salads, smoothies, and aguas frescas. The Río Grande's butcher shop is one of its chief attractions and sells everything from T-bone and ribeye steaks to pork feet and beef tongue. "If you want Cheerios, go to Tom Thumb," advises a regular, "but if you need banana leaves and goat, this is the place." The Río Grande also has a superior seafood section with live catfish, tilapia, and crabs among its selections.

*Movies, Concerts, Exhibits, and Drama*
**Rose Marine Theater**
1440 N. Main St.
Mon.-Fri., 11 a.m.-6 p.m.
817-624-8333
www.artesdelarosa.org

Through the mid-twentieth century, the Rose Marine Theater functioned as a movie house for the Northside's Latino population. Latinos were segregated on the east side of North Main Street, where the Rose Marine was their center of entertainment and a window into the world of Mexican Golden Age film. During the Golden Age, from roughly 1935 to 1960, Mexico dominated the Latin American movie industry with lavish musicals, urban comedies, and dramas depicting rural life. The luminaries of the silver screen periodically came to the Rose Marine, including superstars Cantinflas, Sara García, and Pedro Infante. During his visit, Pedro Infante greeted a long line of well-wishers, accepting kisses and flowers from his admirers. Desegregation and the decay of the Northside's meatpacking plants coincided with the deterioration of Mexican cinema, and the Rose Marine and much of the surrounding neighborhood fell into decline in the 1970s. Eventually the building became a neglected storage facility. In the late 1990s, however, the Rose Marine was restored as part of a larger

Housing and Urban Development project. Today it is listed on the National Register of Historic Places and is home to an active Latino arts center with a packed itinerary of movies, concerts, plays, and exhibitions scheduled throughout the entire year. *Artes de la Rosa* also organizes educational activities, including an award-winning drama program for children. Be sure to visit on Mexican Independence and Day of the Dead, when families fill the beautiful outdoor plaza for a night of music, dance, and celebration.

*Below: The Rose Marine Theater on North Main Street. Next page: Norteño performance at Pequeño México flea market.*

# Música y rumba

Music is one of the most obvious imports to arrive with Latin American immigration to Fort Worth. *Norteño*, *banda*, *ranchera*, and *duranguense* are just a few of the rhythms that can be heard in many stores and restaurants and that occasionally are blasted over car speakers by youthful drivers out for a spin. This section begins with a description of some of the favorite contemporary genres. Next, it turns to bars and clubs that play Latin music and stage live shows. Fort Worth has several superb venues featuring top Mexican entertainers. In addition, there are a number of smaller taverns with lesser-known Tejano and Afro-Cuban acts. Also

*Houston-based Banda Lagunense.*

*Carlos Saenz of Fort Worth's Latin Express.
Photo courtesy of Latin Express.*

listed are several agreeable places for catching a boxing or soccer match or for taking in a rowdy transvestite show. The *show travesti* has become a Fort Worth staple, along with lowriders, jaripeo, and the mariachi band. Latin Americans have invigorated Fort Worth's nightlife. Get out and take advantage of this wonderful contribution.

## Tejano and its Immigrant Competitors

With Selena's rise in the 1990s, Tejano achieved its broadest acceptance, just as thousands of Mexicans faced the disruptions brought on by the im-

plementation of NAFTA and picked up their lives to settle in Texas. Fort Worth's **Stampede** and **Latin Express** continue to crank out Tejano hits, whose bouncy or *bailable* spirit is as grounded in US rhythms as in conventional Mexican music. Nevertheless, most radio stations have now made adjustments and broadcast songs preferred by the newcomers. Some of the principal genres are:

**Norteño** – A product of Central European immigration to the Southwest, the accordion-based *norteño* sounds a lot like polka and recounts stories about the border: its heroes, scoundrels, smugglers, and bandits.

*Mural of Che Guevara inside Embargo.*

**Banda** – *Banda* groups play *corridos*, *boleros*, and other genres, but are defined by their brass and woodwind instruments, blown in a loose, open-throttle manner. To an untrained ear, the music can sound cacophonous, but take the time to appreciate its liberating quality.

**Duranguense** – *Duranguense* is comparable to banda. However, the duranguense pace is much faster and is driven by synthesizers as well as wind instruments.

**Ranchera** – With its dramatic lyrics and melodies, *ranchera* is a kind of New World opera. Ideal for weddings or for drowning your sorrows, it is usually performed by a mariachi ensemble.

**Cumbia** – The most widespread dance music in Latin America, cumbia originates from coastal Colombia and combines light-hearted themes with a distinct galloping beat. *Cumbia* is classic Latin American bus music.

*Caribbean Rhythms*
**Embargo**
210 E. 8th St.
Tues.-Fri., 11 a.m.-2 p.m. and 5 p.m.-2 a.m.; Sat.-Sun., 8 p.m.-2 a.m.; Mon. 5 p.m.-2 a.m.
817-870-9750
www.embargodfw.com

If Fort Worth's large Mexican population influences its Spanish-language musical preferences, this dominance is by no means complete. Indeed the recent fascination with television dance competitions has improved the standing of other rhythms, many of them more closely associated with the Caribbean. Reflecting this shift, the club-restaurant Embargo entertains its customers with hip-swinging salsa, fast-paced merengue and sentimental *bachata*, along with heart-thumping *reggaeton*. Tracks of hip-hop add further excitement to Embargo's weekend environment. The downtown locale engages clients with the most familiar conceptions of Cuba. "If you close your eyes, you can almost hear the waves breaking," remarked a recent Embargo patron. Tropical-themed artwork hangs from rustic walls, and a worn wooden bar provides a comfortable perch for conversing and sipping Cuban mojitos. The mojito is a refreshing beverage, combining white rum with lime juice, sugar, mint, and sparkling water. Outside, the carcass of a 1950s-era automobile decorates the entryway to the establishment. The Embargo hosts weekly salsa lessons, poetry slams, and live musical shows. The kitchen serves up light fare for lunch and continues to operate into the evening when the lights go down and the party begins. Try to look your best when you venture to Embargo. A dress code is en-

*DJ booth at the cavernous Escapade 2001.*

forced, and the vibe borders on swanky. Nearby **Barcelona** (515 Houston Street) provides a similar atmosphere, mixing Caribbean rhythms with hip-hop, cocktails, and fashion.

*Where the Fiesta Never Ends*
**Escapade 2001**
2401 S. Campus Ct.
Fri.-Sun., 8 p.m.-3 a.m.
214-902-6400
www.escapadedallas.com/events/dallasfortworth

With its oversized dance floor, lights, and powerful sound system, Escapade 2001 is an impressive nightspot, enticing thousands of revelers every weekend to whirl about its cavernous environs. Like the OK Corral, the venue features live and recorded music, favoring Mexican genres such as norteño, banda, tribal, and duranguense with occasional blasts of reggaeton and bachata. Escapade 2001 brings leading talent to the Metroplex. Recent visitors have included El Duelo, Los Rieleros del Norte, Bronco, and El Tigrillo Palma. Ramón Ayala, the four-time Grammy-winning accordionist, came to the club in 2012. Patrons favor the postmodern vaquero outfits, now so in vogue among Mexican and Mexican-American youth. Men sport skinny jeans, cowboy hats and shirts, and botas picudas (see p. 55). Tattoos and piercings often complete the look. Women wear heels and short skirts, although virtually every style can be found at the discotheque. On a busy night, expect to be swept away by the crowd, spinning counterclockwise around the gigantic hall and lending it a distinctly communal feel. Escapade 2001 is one of Fort Worth's most active music spots. Consult its website for events and schedules.

*Fútbol Mexicano*
## Liga MX

Without the cachet of European soccer leagues, Liga MX fills stadiums across Mexico and attracts millions of viewers to its televised games. Mexico is, without question, a soccer-mad country, having adopted the sport in the late nineteenth century when British expatriates arrived to pursue economic opportunities and introduced the diversion during their leisure time. The Mexicans gradually developed their own style of play, emphasizing ball control and technique over physicality. In Mexico, there is a deep appreciation for the athlete who can launch rapid attacks, relying on individual skills. The Mexican league was created in 1943. Today it dwarfs its US counterpart, dominating the Confederation of North, Central American, and Caribbean Association Football (CONCACAF)

*Ojos Locos at the corner of Houston and West 5th Streets.*

and other regional competitions. In Fort Worth, *fútbol picante*'s appeal becomes obvious when fans don colorful jerseys and hats and jam into bars to view weekend matches. The season runs from July through May and is divided into an *apertura* (opening) and *clausura* (closing) tournament, each with its own *liguilla* (playoff) and separate champion. Major rivalries include the *Superclásico*, pitting the Yankee-like América of Mexico City against the *Chivas* (Goats) of Guadalajara. The Chivas rely exclusively on Mexican players, and their fans are known as the "sacred herd." A great place to drink a *chela* (brewski) and take in the action is La Gran Plaza's **Las Ranitas** (4200 South Freeway). Downtown's **Ojos Locos** (515 Houston Street) is a Latino version of Hooters with lively crowds gathering for important athletic events. The **South Pump** (5703 Crowley Road) and **Chuyito's Texican Burgers & Cantina** (1521 North Main Street) tend to attract tejano customers who lean more toward the NFL than the Liga MX.

**The Show Travesti**

Transvestite shows have a long history in Mexico and now are quite common in the DFW area. Mexican bars, discos, and restaurants often host the flamboyant artists who imitate singers such as Gloria Trevi, Paquita la del Barrio, Shakira, and Selena. They lip-sync and dance in tight sequin dresses and entertain with their chutzpah and shapely figures. Late-night productions can be especially racy. In the afternoons or early evenings, they are generally tamer, with grandmothers and children among the spectators enthusiastically singing and clapping to the music. The *show travesti* has become a "family" event, insists Gaby Duarte, the head of a local, well-known act, whose imitations incorporate US personalities such as Michael Jackson, Madonna, and Tina Turner. In an interview for *Univision* television, the Salvadoran-born Duarte noted that the

routines are designed to project "fantasy." The idea is to delight with transformations, "to represent oneself as a celebrity and fifteen minutes later to become someone else." In Fort Worth, transvestite shows can be seen on Friday evenings at **Cesar's Tacos** (4728 South Freeway) and on Saturdays at **La Playita** (3025 Cleburne Road). Many other businesses peri-

*Alondra performing as Gloria Trevi at La Playita.*

odically schedule the spectacles, which are usually publicized on the same vibrant handbills that announce musical acts, jaripeos, and similar events.

*The Billy Bob's of Latino Fort Worth*
**OK Corral**
4200 S. Freeway
Fri., 8 p.m.-2 a.m.; Sat., 8 p.m.-3 a.m.; Sun., 8 p.m.-2 a.m.
817-207-0045
www.okcorraldisco.com

Part of a chain of entertainment businesses stretching through Texas and Oklahoma, the OK Corral is Fort Worth's premier club for live Mexican regional music. The main hall hosts norteño, banda, and cumbia performances, usually scheduled on Friday evenings, while the discotheque Babilonia plays rock and reggaeton as well as other Caribbean genres such as salsa, merengue, and bachata. The OK Corral regularly presents major artists such as the legendary Tigres del Norte, Pesado, and Intocable, the Grammy-winning group from Zapata, Texas. Alejandra Guzmán and Joan Sebastian staged concerts in 2011, while "banda diva" Jenni Rivera was an annual highlight until her recent death. Tribal (trēbal) is another feature of the venue. Tribal is a form of electronic music mixing techno recordings with Mexico's traditional rhythms and enveloping

listeners in an extraordinary mix of pulses. Many of the best deejays hail from Monterrey, Mexico, and oversee raucous, oversized parties, with dance competitions between flashily-dressed participants. Women sport high heels and tight-fitting skirts, while the men wear cowboy hats and shirts, skinny jeans, and botas picudas. However you're dressed, be sure to enjoy the OK Corral. Located next to La Gran Plaza, it functions as Fort Worth's Latino Billy Bob's (2520 Rodeo Plaza). For another perspective on Mexican music, pay a visit to the **Cowboy Palace** (160 West Rosedale Street), a more humble club near the hospital district.

*Fort Worth Tejano*
**Neon Nights**
2725 NE 28th St.
Thurs.-Sat., 6 p.m.-2 a.m.
682-647-1552
www.neonnightstexas.com

**Tejano Spurs**
2663 NE 28th St.
Fri. and Sat., 7 p.m.-2 a.m.
817-222-0304
www.tejanospurs.com

Overwhelmed by immigration and the arrival of norteño, duranguense, and other Mexican genres, Tejano struggles to retain a position in Fort Worth's music scene. While its bouncy rhythms remain a part of the soundtrack of South and Central Texas, they are less frequently heard in the DFW area. Two of Cowtown's last Tejano outposts are Neon Nights and Tejano Spurs. Located just blocks from one another, they regularly book bands such as Baraja de Oro, Spanish Fly, Stampede, and Latin Express. The atmosphere at both locales is friendly and unpretentious, approaching that of a country bar. Regulars sport belt buckles and wide-brimmed hats and greet one another like childhood acquaintances. Customers also tend to be older than the patrons at the OK Corral, Barcelona, or Embargo. The clubs schedule periodic cumbia performances, comedians, and occasional karaoke nights. If you find yourself appreciating the music, check out Tony Vasquez's **Tejano Gold Radio** at www.ustream.tv/channel/fort-worth-tejano. Vasquez is a local promoter who organizes Tejano festivals at La Grave Field, usually around Cinco de Mayo. He created his twenty-four-hour online station in response to Tejano's absence on the airways.

## Where to Hire a Good Mariachi Band

Mariachi bands play at restaurants on weekends, brightening the mood with their soaring lyrics, violins, trumpets, and unapologetic panache. More characteristically, they enliven private parties, marking quinceañeras, birthdays, baptisms, and first communions. A walk in Trinity Park can yield an occasional encounter with the musicians sere-

*Below: La Gran Plaza's mariachi academy provides training for young musicians.*

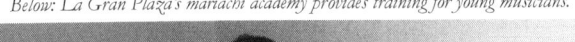

nading guests at picnic barbecues. This author even hired an eight-piece ensemble to help jazz up his wedding ceremony. But where does one look for a good mariachi? It's not as easy as opening the yellow pages. The Internet can provide some assistance, with sites such as GigMasters suggesting a few options. Mariachi de Oro is one of Fort Worth's leading ensembles and has a simple yet useful web site. Most mariachis, however, lack such a presence and must be contacted in a more direct fashion. Probably the place to begin is La Gran Plaza, which hosts ranchera concerts on Saturdays and Sundays and where the artists can be approached when they're on break. The mall's western wear stores often have business cards, as do many of the city's churches. Expect to spend around $500 an hour for a professional group, but college and high school mariachis can be hired for much less. Whatever you

*Below: Mariachi Mexicanísimo at La Gran Plaza.*
*Next page: In Fort Worth, there's a piñata for every occasion.*

do, don't become discouraged. There are dozens of mariachis in the Metroplex, and everyone deserves to experience their mixture of nihilism, grandiosity, and liberating brilliance. Offering a taste of the mariachi experience, **Flamingo's** (1549 North Main Street) and **La Tortilandia** (1112 West Berry Street) have live shows every Friday.

# Calendario Azteca
## Events and Dates

Spiritual and civic celebrations were an essential part of colonial Latin America, helping to legitimize religious and governmental authorities while instilling a sense of shared values amid gaping class and ethnic differences. When the Spanish viceroy, the king's representative, made his appearance in Mexico City, his arrival provoked days of public revelry, drawing slaves, peons, and patricians into a prolonged collective experience. Such festivities also provided opportunities to blow off steam and to lampoon and challenge social elites. The appreciation of the fiesta and its purposes survived the wars of independence and periodic efforts of nineteenth and twentieth-century reformers to rid the region of its perceived excesses. Fort Worth's Latinos seem to preserve this legacy in elaborate picnics on Easter Sunday, in a propensity to gather in restaurants on weekends, and in a willingness among the younger crowd to put aside work and whirl about a dance floor. Radio and newspapers are a good way to stay abreast of the local Latino scene. Tune into **La Raza** (93.7 FM) and **La Bonita** (106.7 FM) and look for copies of *Al Día*,

DFW's free Spanish-language weekly, which regularly posts updates on its excellent web site (www.aldiatx.com).

## Best of Mexico Celebración
Will Rogers Memorial Center
3401 W. Lancaster Ave.
Mid-January
www.fwssr.com

Through most of January and early February, Fort Worth celebrates its annual Stock Show and Rodeo at the Will Rogers Memorial Center. The three-week festival offers an array of competitions, auctions, a parade, and exhibitions, as well as midway rides, food, games, and clinics. A highlight for many is the *Best of Mexico Celebración* with "fourth generation charro" Jerry Diaz. A charro is a traditional horseman, associated with the state of Jalisco and romanticized in Mexico's Golden Age cinema. In the mid-twentieth century, as the country was undergoing urbanization, the movie industry turned nostalgic for earli-

*Diaz's star on the Stockyards' "Texas Trail of Fame," appropriately smeared with horse manure.*

er periods. It portrayed rural life in lavish musical productions such as the classic *Dos Tipos de Cuidado* (1953), starring Jorge Negrete and Pedro Infante. Diaz and his wife Staci revive the glamour of the Golden Age with their elaborate embroidered outfits, their trick roping, and their prancing horses. Like Gene Autry, Jerry sings ballads from the saddle, accompanied by Fort Worth's superb Mariachi de Oro. The Celebración also involves bronc and bull riding and exquisite folkloric dancing. The Escaramuza La Guadalupana, a women's sidesaddle team, dazzles the crowd with its breakneck maneuvers. The Celebración is a one-day event. Consult the Stock Show calendar for the precise date.

## Golden Gloves Regional and State Tournaments
Will Rogers Memorial Center
3401 W. Lancaster Ave.
Mid-February to early March
817-336-1313
www.texasgoldengloves.com

A week before Stevie Cruz's fight in Las Vegas, his father etched "World Champion" in the fresh cement outside his modest Diamond Hill residence. Cruz defeated his opponent in the 1986 match to claim the World Boxing Association (WBA) featherweight crown. The triumph, which was celebrated with a parade through the Northside, highlighted a remarkable local sporting tradition, yielding dozens of national Golden Gloves victories and five world titles among the professional ranks. Boxing has deep roots in Fort Worth, especially among the Latino community, whose heroes include Vanessa Juarez, a former standout at the amateur level and a pioneer in the growth of female pugilism. Today, the city's boxing competitions regularly have women fighters. One of the best ways to appreciate these sporting legacies is to attend the annual Golden Gloves Tournament, which begins in mid-February and runs through early March. The tour-

*Golden Gloves Gym—1972 George Barton Award*

nament, which was first held in 1936, draws participants from around the state and attracts a large and spirited audience. Fort Worth also hosts occasional professional contests, many of them organized by Paulie Ayala at LaGrave Field or at the convention center. Ayala is another local hero who won the WBA bantamweight belt in 1999.

### Lent and Comida de Cuaresma

Lent commemorates the forty days Jesus spent in the desert before the start of his ministry. The observance runs for about six weeks, from Ash Wednesday to shortly before Easter. Catholics, who end Lent on Holy Thursday, regard this period as a time of penance, prayer, almsgiving, fasting, and abstinence. They traditionally give up a preferred food or amenity, and they refrain from eating meat

*Lenten meals advertised outside Fiesta Mexican Restaurant (3233 Hemphill St.).*

on Fridays. In Mexico and elsewhere, these spiritual obligations have given rise to a special cuisine, which is considered by some as less of a sacrifice and more as a long-awaited gratification. "The menu reads 'it's time to be good,' but I think of it as an opportunity for great cooking," observed a fan of the religious season. Mexican restaurants prepare *comida de cuaresma* (Lenten food), including fish dishes, shrimp and spinach *tortitas* (patties), *chiles rellenos* (stuffed peppers), lentil soup, and *nopalitos*. Nopalitos are the diced pads of the prickly pear cactus, and they usually arrive in a light tomato broth. Also common are *romeritos*, a rosemary-like herb that tastes like spinach and which is served with potatoes in *mole* sauce. For desert, order the syrupy *capirotada*, a bread pudding featuring raisins and walnuts, *piloncillo* (unrefined sugar), cheese, cloves, and cinnamon. The sweet, tangy combination is a delight to the taste buds and appeases the stomachs of those forgoing meat. The **Acapulco Restaurant** is located at 1320 NW 25th Street and advertises itself as "No. 1 for Lent."

## Easter Sunday in Trinity Park
2401 University Drive

Visitors to Mexico have often commented on the enthusiastic use of marketplaces, streets, plazas,

*Confetti-filled* cascarones *are another feature of Easter.*

and similar spaces to chat, fraternize, and to see and be seen. Muralist Diego Rivera captured this mixing in a 1948 depiction of Mexico City. Rivera's fresco offers a vision of the late nineteenth and early twentieth centuries, portraying the period as an assortment of aristocrats, lowlifes, rebels, tyrants, and other characters strolling about the capital's Alameda Park. The same urge to congregate has transferred to Fort Worth with the arrival of Mexican immigrants. Indeed, places such as the Southside's Capps Park (907 West Berry Street) are filled with people in the evenings: joggers and others out for a casual walk, grandparents, children, and the ubiquitous paleta carts. On weekends, the grounds tend to be especially crowded with an endless series of *fútbol* matches. The mingling ethic, however, is most on display in Trinity Park on Easter Sunday. There, hundreds of families celebrate the holiday over barbecues, games, and norteño music. Inflatable "jump-castles" are a frequent sight, as are balloons and *papel picado*, the intricately cut banners made of colored tissue paper. Immigration has revitalized Fort Worth's recreational areas, transforming these quiet and once-ignored settings into lively arenas of socialization.

*Vending stand at All Saints Cinco de Mayo festival.*

### Cinco de Mayo at All Saints Catholic Church
214 NW 20th St.
817-626-3055

Fort Worth residents eagerly embrace the annual Cinco de Mayo activities, flocking to bars and restaurants to enjoy Mexican food, margaritas, and cold *cerveza*. Some businesses hire *conjunto* and mariachi groups to invigorate further the festive environment. The city's best Cinco de Mayo fiesta is hosted by the Northside's All Saints Catholic Church. The weekend carnival features a parade, games, vendors, and an evening dance with a boisterous cumbia/norteño band. Expect to be enveloped in the hip-swinging rhythms spinning couples about the dance floor. The revelry marks the anniversary of Mexico's 1862 victory over the French at Puebla. Napoleon III had sent troops into the country with the aim of creating a puppet monarchy, and while they eventually installed Maximilian I, the early defeat of one of the world's most powerful armies gave a morale boost to the Mexicans, all too familiar with foreign conquests. Ultimately, Maximilian was unable to establish his legitimacy and died before a firing squad in 1867. Today Cinco de Mayo is more widely observed in the United States than in Mexico, and the holiday has taken on a significance comparable to St. Patrick's Day for Irish-Americans. For many, it's about expressing pride in one's ancestry. A nostalgic ranchera, heard at parties, captures its importance for those of Mexican descent: "My beautiful and beloved Mexico/ should I die far from you/ let them say I'm asleep/ and bring me back to you."

**¡Viva México!**
La Gran Plaza
4200 S. Freeway
September 15 and 16
817-922-8888
www.lagranplazamall.com

*Independence bell on the balcony of La Gran Plaza.*

Mexican independence is enthusiastically commemorated in Fort Worth and other parts of the Metroplex. Central to the festivities is the reenactment of Father Miguel Hidalgo's *Grito* (Cry) that initiated the revolt against Spanish colonialism on September 16, 1810. Hidalgo was a brilliant and unconventional priest who had been assigned to a small town in Guanajuato for his enlightened, unorthodox thinking and his insistence on living with the mother of his children. He began the rebellion in the early morning hours, ordering the ringing of the church bells and addressing his followers on the steps of the parish church. Hidalgo was a poor military leader, however, and he soon was captured and faced execution. Nevertheless, his rebellion began a decade-long struggle culminating in the definitive break from Spain in 1821. Tributes to the Grito traditionally take place at 11 p.m. on September 15. Mexico's president and leaders across the republic laud the heroes of independence and ring bells and wave flags from government buildings. In Fort Worth, La Gran Plaza hosts an animated gala with the Mexican consul general directing the ceremonies from a balcony overlooking the mall's central square. Be sure to participate in the call-and-response *Vivas*. When the official belts out, "Long Live Mexico," brace your lungs and join the crowd's bone-rattling *Viva*!

## TCU Latin American Music Festival

TCU Campus
Late September-early October (every two years)
817-257-7143
www.latinarts.tcu.edu

*German Gutiérrez and the TCU Symphony. Photo courtesy of Paul Cortese.*

Since 1996, Germán A. Gutiérrez has served as TCU's director of orchestras, taking the program to a new level of excellence while giving it a distinct Latino orientation. The Colombian-born Gutiérrez recruits students from across Latin America and accepts regular invitations to conduct in the region, and the TCU symphony has recently staged concerts in Puerto Rico as part of its Festival Iberoamericano. In 2011, the orchestra won the prestigious *Premio Gardel* for its collaboration with Opus Cuatro, a vocal quartet that traveled from Argentina to record an album in Fort Worth.

The emphasis on rhythms south of the border takes an especially obvious turn every two years, when Gutiérrez and his colleagues sponsor the Latin American Music Festival. The weeklong event includes TCU students interpreting pieces by Latin American composers, as well as concerts by prominent visiting artists. In 2011, TCU showcased the Chilean guitarist Luis Orlandi, Colombian-Spanish soprano Patricia Caicedo, Puerto Rico-based trombonist Luis Fred, and the Colombian folk group Guafa Trío. The next Latin American Music Festival will be held in fall 2016. Check the TCU website for the schedule. All events are free.

### Fiestalorico and Mexican Folk Dance
October-November
Ballet Folklórico Azteca (www.bfazteca.com)
Ballet Folklórico de Fort Worth (on Facebook)
Sol de Fort Worth Ballet Folklórico (www.solfw.com)

*Performance of the* jarana yucateca *by the Ballet Folklórico Azteca. Photo courtesy of J.D. Vordokas.*

In the mid-twentieth century, Amalia Hernández founded the Ballet Folklórico de México, standardizing and choreographing regional dances into a moving display of nationalism. Today Hernández's company performs every Wednesday and Sunday in Mexico City's ornate Palacio de Bellas Artes, while less prestigious troupes present her compositions in other communities across Mexico and the United States. Among the Mexican American population, the shows evoke a sense of ethnic solidarity. Fort Worth boasts several Mexican dance groups, the oldest of which was founded in 1975 and today is based out of La Gran Plaza (4200 South Freeway, Suite 1830). The Ballet Folklórico Azteca and its competitors (Ballet Folklórico de Fort Worth and Sol de Fort Worth Ballet Folklórico) participate in events such as Mayfest and the Mainstreet Arts Festival. They take part in contests around the region and provide occasional entertainment in hospitals. Dancers range in age from toddlers to young adults and sport the charming costumes that typify the genre. For an introduction to the beauty of Mexican dance, consider attending Fiestalorico, a day-long recital hosted by Ballet Folklórico Azteca. Fiestalorico draws talent from across Texas and culminates with appearances by professional artists; check the Ballet Folklórico Azteca website for dates and times. All three Fort

Worth schools offer affordable classes for those interested in Mexican dance.

## El Día de los Muertos (Day of the Dead)
Rose Marine Theater
1440 N. Main St.
November 1-2
817-624-8333
www.artesdelarosa.org

El Día de los Muertos perhaps constitutes the most iconic occasion on the Mexican calendar. The holiday combines pre-Hispanic religious practices, including veneration of the dead, with the Catholic traditions that arrived with the Conquest. Such mixing or syncretism is typical of all religions; however, it becomes especially evident in Mexican communities on the Catholic feasts of All Saints and All Souls (November 1 and 2). On these days, many families visit cemeteries and clean the graves of deceased relatives, decorating their tombs with marigold flowers, *calaveras* (skull candies), candles, drinks, and food items enjoyed by the loved ones during their lives. The *angelitos* (children) are honored on November 1, while adults receive their commemoration on November 2. Some people also erect elaborate home altars, adorned with gifts

Día de los Muertos *at the Rose Marine Theater.*

for the departed who are thought to commune with
the living during these hours. In Fort Worth, El Día
de los Muertos is marked with several public celebrations, including a wonderful open-air bazaar at
the Rose Marine Theater. The nighttime gathering
includes a skull parade, mariachis, folk dancing, and

art exhibitions. All events are well attended. Arrive early and bring a blanket or lawn chairs.

## Saint Cecilia and the Blessing of the Mariachis

La Gran Plaza
4200 S. Freeway
Late November
817-922-8888
www.lagranplazamall.com

*Fort Worth's Flor del Rocío on La Gran Plaza's stage.*

In a well-known song, Vicente Fernández describes himself as "surrounded by mariachis" and suffering from the tumult they provoke in his heart. The mariachi is a musical ensemble with violins, trumpets, and guitars, as well as a bass instrument known as a *guitarrón*. The smaller but similarly shaped *vihuela* adds a sharp sense of rhythm and is sometimes accompanied by a harp. Members of the mariachi also sing, usually in a forceful, almost operatic manner. The arrangement originated in nineteenth-century Jalisco and today is viewed as Mexico's most recognizable music. In Fernández's piece, the narrator drinks a tequila and requests that the band play his ex-lover's favorites. Quickly he descends into a state of despondence and croons mournfully, "Drunk, I remember you." If mariachis can evoke pride, humor, and happiness, they are especially adept at conjuring the misery evident in Vicente Fernández's lyrics. Like the blues or country music, they can dwell on tragedies, and with their flamboyance and blasting horns, create a sense of catharsis. "There are birds," Fernández asserts in another tale of disillusionment, "that cross the marsh without getting wet . . . and you know that I am of that plumage." In Fort Worth, the best way to become familiar with this Mexican treasure is to attend La Gran Plaza's "Blessing of the Mariachis." The blessing coincides roughly with the feast of Saint Cecilia (November 22), the Catholic patroness of music, and involves presentations by local groups. Father Stephen Jasso of All Saints Catholic Church oversees the religious segment of the festivities.

## Tamales and Christmas in Fort Worth
December

If Fort Worthians prefer turkey and pumpkin pie on Thanksgiving, they hanker for fresh tamales

during the Christmas season. Tamales are an important festival food in Mexico, dating back to the pre-Hispanic period, and they have become wildly popular in the Metroplex through the month of December. Fort Worth churches organize tamale fundraisers, as do schools, TCU sororities, and families. Non-Latinos have eagerly taken up the custom and make tamales for sale or for their own consumption. Don't be surprised by the courteous tamale vendors who may approach as you exit the supermarket. Sellers stake out these and other high traffic areas, waiting to meet potential buyers. Tamales are *masa* (corn dough) stuffed with chicken, pork, cheese, chiles, or vegetables. They are wrapped in corn husks and then steamed, with the husks removed before they are eaten. Normally tamales are sold by the dozen. There are innumerable locations to buy these holiday staples, ranging from **Central Market** (4651 West Freeway) to (potentially) your next-door neighbor. Pickup trucks often hawk them at busy intersections. **Hot Damn Tamales** (713 West Magnolia Avenue) prepares a variety of "gourmet" versions, while **Mi Cocinita** (3509 ½ Bryan Avenue) has earned a reputation for producing some of the best traditional tamales.

### Feast of Our Lady of Guadalupe

Saint Patrick Cathedral
1206 Throckmorton St.
December 12
817-332-4915
www.stpatrickcathedral.org

Our Lady of Guadalupe Church
4100 Blue Mound Rd.
817-626-7421
www.fwolg.com

*Shrine to Guadalupe at Esperanza's Restaurant.*

On December 12, Catholics across Mexico gather in churches in the early morning hours to mark the feast of Our Lady of Guadalupe. The Virgin Mary's apparition in 1531 on a hillside outside Mexico City has long been a central component of Mexican identity. Her arrival occurred on the heels of the Conquest, which had ravaged Mexico and forced Christianity on its inhabitants. Guadalupe came as a brown-skinned woman. She spoke the native Náhuatl language and directed herself to an indigenous peasant, instead of addressing a Spanish official. For Mexicans, her appearance constituted a vindication. She demonstrated that Mexicans had their own connection to Christ and that there was no justification for the Europeans' impositions and violence. In the United States, Guadalupe's story resounds powerfully among immigrants and speaks to their own difficulties and social marginalization. She is the defender of the underdog, the powerless, and the undocumented. The services in her honor are elaborate affairs and typically involve mariachis and *matachines* (pre-Hispanic dancers). While the dancers validate Mexican identity, the mariachis serenade Guadalupe on her feast day. In Fort Worth, **Saint Patrick Cathedral** and **Our Lady of Guadalupe Church** offer some of the most joyful masses.

# Gringo's Glossary

Still confused about *bolillos*, *birria*, *buche*, and *botánicas*, or perplexed by what distinguishes a *huarache* from a *chalupa*? Below is a list of expressions and terms to help gringos and gringas order their breakfasts, to make meat selections for their *tortas* and *tacos*, and to understand the varieties of Spanish-language music. Fort Worth has a rich Latino heritage. Language should be no impediment to embracing it.

*Aguas frescas at El Río Grande juice bar.*

*A la veracruzana*: Veracruz style. A tomato-based sauce with capers, olives, oregano, jalapeños, and garlic. Often used to prepare fish and other seafood.

*Aguas frescas*: Fresh waters. A non-alcoholic drink made of water and blended fruits, flowers, or seeds. *Aguas frescas* are served from giant glass jars.

*Artesanías*: Handicrafts, ranging from textiles, baskets, paintings, and pottery to religious items, tiles, statuary, and furniture.

*Bachata*: Sentimental Dominican music with distinctive plucking guitars and with lyrics recounting tales of heartache and loss.

*Bajito y suavecito*: Low and slow, the longstanding motto of the lowrider scene.

*Banda*: A genre of Mexican regional music, uniting brass, woodwind, and percussion instruments into a loose explosion of sound.

*Barbacoa*: Slow-cooked, tender meat, often from the head of a cow. A favorite for tacos, burritos, and tortas.

*Break time outside Banda Lagunense bus.*

**Béisbol**: Baseball.

**Birria**: Savory goat or lamb stew, sometimes with bones and tendons.

**Bolillo**: Shorter version of the French baguette, with a crispy exterior crust and a soft center. Also called *pan francés* (French bread).

**Botánica**: Shop specializing in the sale of alternative religious and curative products. Also known as a *hierbería* or *yerbería* in reference to medicinal herbs (*hierbas*).

**Botas picudas**: Pointy boots. Extravagantly long and decorated boots worn by young males for dancing to *tribal*, a hybrid musical fusion of techno with *cumbia* and other rhythms.

**Buche**: Pork stomach.

**Cabeza**: Beef head.

**Cabrito**: Roast kid goat, typical of the northern Mexican city of Monterrey.

**Calaveras**: Colorful representations of the human skull, usually in clay or sugar form. An important decorative element of *Día de los Muertos*.

**Caldo**: Soup.

**Campechana**: Glazed and flakey rectangular pastry, filled with cream or fruit jams.

**Capirotada**: Bread pudding made for the Lenten season.

**Carne asada**: Grilled steak.

**Carne guisada**: Stew meat.

**Carnitas**: Shredded pork or beef.

**Cemita**: A vaguely sweet sesame-seed roll. Sandwiches using this roll are also *cemitas*.

**Ceviche**: Raw seafood cured in citrus juices and flavored with onions, salt, chiles, and cilantro. Frequently eaten with saltine crackers.

**Chalupa**: Thin and crunchy *masa* base with meats, cheese, salsa, and vegetables. Resembles a *chalupa*, a small, narrow boat.

**Chamoy**: A spicy, sweet and sour fruit sauce, similar to chutney in taste and texture.

**Chamoyada**: Snow cone with fruit, powdered chile, and *chamoy*. Gummy bears are occasionally added to the mix.

**Charro**: Horseman from central-western Mexico, particularly from the state of Jalisco. Famous for elegant, silver-studded suits and for participation in the *charreada* rodeo.

**Chela**: Cold beer.

***Chicharrón***: Fried pork rinds.

***Chilaquiles***: Fried corn tortilla strips with salsa and cheese, sometimes combined with scrambled eggs or chicken. Similar to *migas*.

***Chile verde***: Pork or beef stew in green chile sauce.

***Chiles rellenos***: Stuffed roasted peppers. Popular during the Lenten season.

***Chimenea***: Earthenware fire pit with rounded base and vertical chimney. A legacy of pre-Hispanic Mexico and now a standard patio item.

***Chorizo***: Sausage.

***Churros***: Elongated fried-dough pastry, sprinkled with sugar.

***Comida de Cuaresma***: Lenten food. Fish, shrimp and spinach *tortitas* (patties), *chiles rellenos* (stuffed peppers), and *nopalitos* are just a few of the options.

***Concha***: Round sweet bun covered with a sugary-crusty shell (*concha*). *Conchas* can be pink, yellow, white, and brown.

***Cumbia***: One of the most widespread musical genres of Latin America. *Cumbia* originates from Colombia and boasts a distinct galloping beat.

***Curandero (m.), curandera (f.)***: Healer who relies on alternative medicinal and spiritual practices.

***Curtido***: Fermented cabbage salad served with *pupusas*.

***Día de los Muertos***: Day of the Dead, October 31-November 2. Iconic Mexican religious festival corresponding to All Hallows' Eve and All Saints and All Souls Days.

***Duranguense***: Type of Mexican regional music associated with the state of Durango. Much like *banda*, but faster-paced and reliant on synthesizers.

***Elote***: Náhuatl-related word meaning corn on the cob. Grilled or boiled *elote* is a common street food.

***Empanada***: Crescent-shaped turnover packed with meats, cheeses, and vegetables, or with sweet fillings such as pumpkin, yam, or fruit.

***Flauta***: Literally, a flute. Fried and tightly rolled

flour tortilla with meat and/or cheese contents.

**_Fútbol_**: Soccer. Also called _fútbol soccer_ to distinguish it from _fútbol americano_—US-style football.

**_Gordita_**: Little fatty. A thick corn cake crammed with a variety of meats and vegetables.

**_Guisado_**: Stew.

**_Guitarrón_**: Six-string bass instrument in mariachi groups. _Guitarrón_ is a large guitar.

**_Huarache_**: Flattened and fried _masa_ topped with salsa, meat, cheese, and vegetables. Named after a kind of Mexican sandal (_huarache_) and bigger than the _sope_, _chalupa_, and _tostada_.

**_Jamaica_**: Church fundraiser involving food and entertainment.

**_Jaripeo_**: Form of Mexican rodeo featuring bull riding.

**_Jarrón_**: Large ceramic jug or vase.

**_Lengua_**: Beef tongue for tacos, tortas, and other dishes.

*Bucking chute at the Plaza México.*

**Loroco**: Edible flower native to Central America, cooked in Salvadoran *pupusas*. *Loroco* tastes a bit like asparagus.

**Machito**: Roasted goat innards.

**Mariachi**: Quintessential Mexican musical ensemble, identified with the state of Jalisco, with guitars, violins, and trumpets, as well as an operatic style of singing.

**Mariscos**: Seafood.

**Masa**: Corn dough used to make tortillas and tamales.

**Matachines**: Fantastically dressed members of indigenous dance groups who perform for religious celebrations such as the Feast of the Virgen de Guadalupe.

**Menudo**: Beef-stomach soup, traditionally prepared on weekends and regarded as a cure for headaches and hangovers.

**Mercado**: Market.

**Merengue**: Fast-paced Dominican dance music, now popular across the Spanish-speaking world.

**Metate**: Rectangular stone for grinding corn in Mesoamerica.

**Michelada**: Bloody Mary-like drink combining beer, lime juice, Tabasco, soy, and Worcestershire sauces. The *michelada* is thought to alleviate hangovers.

**Migas**: Breakfast plate whose primary ingredients include scrambled eggs and strips of tortillas.

**Milanesa**: Breaded cutlet, served in sandwiches or

on its own.

***Mojito***: Refreshing Cuban concoction blending white rum with lime juice, sugar, mint, and sparkling water.

***Molcajete***: Stone vessel for grinding spices. Now a serving bowl in many restaurants.

***Mole***: Chile- and chocolate-based sauce, common in Mexican cuisine.

***Moño***: Sweet bread in the pattern of a bow (*moño*).

***Muralismo***: Muralism. Artistic movement associated with Mexican Revolution and with painted murals on government buildings. Later embraced by Mexican-American communities.

***Náhuatl***: Language of the Aztec Empire and today Mexico's most important Native American linguistic group, with over two dozen varieties and some one million speakers, extending into Central America.

***Nopalitos***: Diced pads of the prickly pear cactus, eaten in salads, with eggs, and in sauces.

***Norteño***: Accordion-based music that sounds a lot like polka and relates the dramas of the border.

*Baked goods on display at Joe T. Garcia's.*

**Novia**: Sweet bread found in Mexican bakeries. Circular in shape and dusted with sugar. Means girlfriend or bride.

**Oreja**: Flat and flaky sweet pastry. Looks like an ear (*oreja*).

**Pachuco**: Member of the flamboyant youth culture that flourished in the Southwest in the mid-twentieth century and is associated with the zoot suit.

**Paleta**: Milk or water popsicle made with fresh fruit.

**Paletero**: Popsicle vendor, often mounted on a bicycle.

**Panadería**: Bakery. Often sells breakfasts and lunches, as well as baked goods.

**Pan de muerto**: Bread of the dead. Sweet roll for *Día de los Muertos*, sometimes featuring skull and bone designs.

**Papel picado**: Intricately cut tissue paper, used as decoration, frequently depicting Day of the Dead themes.

**Pelotero**: Baseball player.

**Piloncillo**: Unrefined cane sugar, molded into a cone.

**Pollo**: Chicken.

**Polvorón**: Powdery, pecan-flavored cookie. Favorite at weddings.

**Las Posadas**: Celebration held during the nine days before Christmas, commemorating Joseph and Mary's trip to Bethlehem and their search for a room. *Posada* means inn.

***Pregones***: Shouts of street vendors. Incorporated periodically into music.

***Pupusa***: Thick corn tortilla, stuffed with *loroco*, pork, cheese, and/or refried beans. The *pupusa* is a Salvadoran dish and comes with a cabbage slaw called *curtido*.

***Quinceañera***: Observance to mark a girl's fifteenth birthday with a religious ceremony and fiesta.

***Ranchera***: Passionate music played by mariachi bands, glorifying the countryside and rural life while exploring human loss, disillusionment, and triumph.

***Raspado***: Snow cone.

***Reggaeton***: Caribbean music, developed in Puerto Rico and Panama, which draws heavily on dance-hall and hip-hop.

***Regiomontano***: That which comes from the Mexican city of Monterrey.

**Roles de canela**: Cinnamon rolls. Also called *rollos de canela*.

**Romeritos**: Rosemary-like herb served with potato and shrimp patties in a rich *mole* sauce. Prepared for Christmas and Lent.

**Rosca de reyes**: Circular fruit cake eaten on Epiphany (January 6). Each king cake contains a small figurine, representative of Baby Jesus.

**Salsa**: Caribbean musical genre which arose in New York in the 1970s and which evolved out of *son* and other Afro-Cuban rhythms.

**Show travesti**: Transvestite show.

**Sincronizada**: Ham and melted cheese between two flour tortillas. A tortilla sandwich.

**Sobador**: Practitioner of a massage therapy to assuage sprains, aches, tension, and migraines.

**Sopa marinera**: Seafood soup.

**Supermercado**: Supermarket.

***Tacos al pastor***: Shepherds tacos. Marinated, spit-grilled pork tacos, a legacy of Middle Eastern immigration and the adaptation of the shawarma to a Mexican context. Similar to the gyro or the kebab.

***Talavera***: Colorful glazed pottery from Puebla, Mexico.

***Tamale***: Corn dough (*masa*) with meats and vegetables, wrapped in corn husks, and steamed until firm. A holiday favorite.

***Taquito***: Little taco. Fried and tightly rolled, corn tortilla with meat and/or cheese interior.

***Tianguis***: Náhuatl-derived word for open-air market.

***Tornillo***: Screw. Spiral pastry filled with custard.

***Torta***: Juicy Mexican sandwich with French-style baguette, called the *bolillo*.

***Tortillería***: Business which specializes in making tortillas.

***Tortitas***: Patties, popular during the Lenten season, especially those made of potato, spinach, shrimp, and tuna.

**Tres leches cake**: Three milk cake. Sponge cake saturated with evaporated milk, condensed milk, and heavy cream.

**Tribal**: Hybrid form of electronic music blending techno with cumbia and Mexican regional music.

**Trío**: Ensemble of three vocalist-guitarists who perform romantic songs.

**Tripas**: Small intestines prepared for tacos, tortas, and burritos.

**Tronco**: Trunk. Cylinder cake with inner swirls of chocolate, jam, and/or cream.

**Vaquero**: Horseman or cowboy.

**Vihuela**: Five-string, guitar-like instrument used in mariachi bands.

**Yoyo**: Mexican sweet bread resembling a yo-yo, usually packed with raspberry jelly.

# About Peter Szok

Peter Szok is a graduate of Tulane University, where he received a PhD in modern Latin American history and specialized in ethnicity, nationalism, and popular culture. Szok is a professor of history at TCU, where he teaches classes in Afro-Latin American history, indigenous movements, and Central America.